Endor

In *Real Writing*, five teachers invite you ⎯ ⎯⎯⎯⎯⎯ᴠꜱation about writing essays: how complex and unique and beautifully crafted they can be. These wise teachers show that joy and rigor are dependent on curiosity—in students and in teachers—as their own critical thinking about teaching is made visible. You will find much to think about here. Enjoy this important journey.

—Penny Kittle, English teacher and author of *Write Beside Them*

Real Writing: Modernizing the Old School Essay makes the bold arguments that our students will become more engaged in the art of composing and that they will develop identities as powerful essayists when they are encouraged to produce real texts for authentic audiences and purposes. As English teachers we need to heed their call; today's youth have so many valuable contributions to make to the larger world of ideas and it is our professional and moral responsibility to cultivate and affirm their unique and beautiful voices. Toward this noble end, the authors have presented us with an honest and thoughtful guide to revolutionizing the teaching of writing in the age of digital participatory culture. Essays, they remind us, are key artifacts in the manifestation of civic society and the act of writing them an essential civil literacy. I am inspired by their words to become a better teacher and a more audacious and prolific composer myself.

—Ernest Morrell, Teachers College, Columbia University.

Pity the essay. Few forms carry the stigma of school writing like that thing we call the "essay," particularly in its 5-paragraph form. Yet in the wild, the essayist tradition of exploration and argument amuses and delights, finding its place in magazines, short films, civic arguments, and cultural criticism of all types. It is the very medium of thought. The authors of *Real Writing: Modernizing the Old School Essay* urge us to liberate the essay from the constraints we as teachers artificially place on it so that it take up the passion and complexity that makes it worth reading and, for students, makes it worth writing. That's what they have done, and in this practical and readable book they show us how we can do it as well.

—Elyse Eidman-Aadahl, executive director, National Writing Project

Real Writing: Modernizing the Old School Essay is an accessible and eye-opening book. It reminds educators why the essay is so much more than a boring formality today. Instead, through practical examples and hands on activities, *Real Writing* reveals how to make composition *vital* and necessary in our classrooms. Challenging what writing looks like, who it's for, and how to make it more impactful than any formulaic five-paragraph example could ever hope, *Real Writing* is a call-to-arms for instructors everywhere; it guides us to take a solid look at what just might be the secret weapon for student engagement in our classrooms today.

—Antero Garcia, assistant professor of English, Colorado State University

Real Writing

Modernizing the Old School Essay

Mitchell Nobis, Daniel Laird, Carrie Nobis,
Dawn Reed, and Dirk Schulze

ROWMAN & LITTLEFIELD
Lanham • Boulder • New York • London

Published by Rowman & Littlefield
A wholly owned subsidiary of The Rowman & Littlefield Publishing Group, Inc.
4501 Forbes Boulevard, Suite 200, Lanham, Maryland 20706
www.rowman.com

Unit A, Whitacre Mews, 26-34 Stannary Street, London SE11 4AB

British Library Cataloguing in Publication Information Available

Library of Congress Cataloging-in-Publication Data Available
ISBN 9781475824780 (cloth : alk. paper)
ISBN 9781475824797 (pbk. : alk. paper)
ISBN 9781475824803 (electronic)

♾™ The paper used in this publication meets the minimum requirements of American
National Standard for Information Sciences—Permanence of Paper for Printed Library
Materials, ANSI/NISO Z39.48-1992.

Printed in the United States of America

To Carrie

*for supporting me in every way and for challenging me to be
a better teacher, father, husband, and human.*

—M.N.

To Mitch

for being my ideal personal and professional teammate.

—C.N.

To Kelsey

*for reminding me what is important
and supporting me anyway with whatever I do when I forget*

—D.L.

To Michael

*who reminds me to keep it real
and for all those that work for social justice and encourage civic engagement.*

—D.R.

To my parents,

*because the best teaching begins with love, with joy, and with patience,
and they have, every year, modeled this for me.*

—D.S.

Contents

Foreword

As I read *Real Writing: Modernizing the Old School Essay*, I kept thinking to myself: FINALLY!

Finally, a sensible and wise book that takes on what we could call "the salience of the traditional" when it comes to well-meaning but unhelpful and even misconceived writing instruction.

Finally, a book that is grounded in the authority of actual classroom practice that demonstrates the options for promoting real world writing—with all its joys and struggles, challenges and satisfactions.

Finally, a book that promotes moving away from the "schoolish" and toward what cognitive scientists call "the correspondence concept," the notion that we need to teach students to do what real experts do in the real world, and that instruction must move students toward expertise and down the correspondence continuum by having them practice doing what real experts, readers, and writers do.

Finally, a book that explores the importance of teaching rhetorical stance and situation and explores how context informs how a piece must be crafted.

Finally, a book that explores the difference between argument and persuasion.

As I read this book, my "FINALLYs" were punctuated by several "BRAVOs!"

Bravo for promoting arguments and essays that require hard thinking about issues that matter, and that tell the story of that thinking.

Bravo for bravely and compassionately taking on the five paragraph essay and all forms of formulaic writing in favor of teaching the kinds of composing that are extremely challenging, but also exciting to do, that are filled with voice and energy and even joy.

Bravo for demonstrating how to create classroom contexts and activities that will assist students over time to be inducted into the strategic repertoire of expert composers.

Bravo for exploring how to create inquiry contexts for writing, and for modeling how to create inquiry-oriented instructional assistance. Bravo especially for the intelligent consideration of invention: how to help students generate topics and material worth writing about.

Finally, a book that offers challenges and solutions not only to what and how we teach when it comes to writing, especially argument, but also to what counts, and why this counts, and how to assess what we say we value.

This book is immensely practical, but it's about big ideas too. It's about personal and communal responsibility. It's about how evidentiary reasoning needs to be the basis of personal as well as democratic decision making.

Another big idea: argument is about creating knowledge and furthering understanding versus winning. Argument is entering into a conversation, and is about working hard to see all perspectives and take them seriously.

This book achieves all this without simplifying the profound expertise that is required to be a successful teacher of composition and a composer of arguments and essays. I found myself thinking several times of the Tom Hanks character in *A League of Their Own* telling the Geena Davis character: "It's the hard that makes it good!"

Here's my major takeaway: We all need to be better arguers, better readers of argument, and people who are willing to act on arguments that are compelling because of their evidence and reasoning. That will take better and more wide-awake teaching of argument. And this book is a wonderful thinking partner for achieving this goal of better teaching of real writing.

As the authors themselves write: "Quite literally for the sake of a functional society and a livable planet, we need to assure that the next generations are better at assessing and analyzing evidence. They need to be better at determining what needs to be done."

Finally! Bravo!

—Jeffrey D. Wilhelm
Distinguished Professor of English Education, Boise State University,
and author of *You Gotta BE the Book, Reading Don't Fix No Chevys*,
and numerous other books about literacy and literacy learning

Acknowledgments

Although only five of us collaborated to write this book, the support of many others was instrumental in bringing it to fruition, and so we express our gratitude to those who helped and encouraged us along the way.

We are grateful for the National Writing Project and its support of teachers teaching teachers and of teachers engaging in their own writing. Janet Swenson, former director of Red Cedar Writing Project at Michigan State University, you connected and mentored us, and we thank you. We are indebted to all of the teacher consultants of Red Cedar Writing Project and Northern Virginia Writing Project.

We thank our students who were willing to share their work with others, our colleagues and mentors who have encouraged our work and inspired our thinking, and those who have partnered in writing for real audiences: Paul Allison, Chris Sloan, and Karen Fasimpaur of Youth Voices; and Annelise Wunderlich and Matt Williams for their work at KQED. Thank you also to Elizabeth Cyr and Aram Kabodian for sharing their work with others.

This book would not exist without Sarah Jubar, our editor at Rowman and Littlefield, who recognized that we had something special to share with other teachers. Thank you as well to the entire Rowman and Littlefield team for their work in helping our ideas reach a new audience.

Special thanks go to Jeffrey Wilhelm for writing our foreword and supporting authentic writing opportunities for all learners.

We're grateful for our families who supported this work: Our parents who got us here; our children—Charlie and Franklin, Harper and Maya, Callie and Gracie—may they too embrace the real power of writing; and Kelsey, Lisa, and Michael, who understood that we were really doing work when laughter, *Star Wars* references, or basketball jokes were the sounds of our writing time.

To name all of the individual teachers and writers who helped us become the educators we are would be impossible, but we want to take a moment to thank all of those colleagues who treated us as professionals, who encouraged us to teach and to learn, and who showed us how to share our expertise with others. That this book exists is testament to your words, your time, and your continuing influence. Thank you.

Introduction

Writing is hard. Let's get that out of the way right up front. Even paid, professional writers bemoan the act of sitting down to write. There's an old procrastinators' joke that the laundry would never get done if it weren't for writing deadlines. This doesn't mean that writing isn't worth doing, of course. The fact that you're holding this book means you're probably a writing instructor, and there are good odds that means you've had your life changed in some way by reading. The beauty of words in fiction, poetry, essays, and a thousand other genres is exactly what drew most writing teachers to this job in the first place. We love words, and so we love writing, despite its difficulty.

But if writing is hard, teaching writing is even harder. In fact, it can seem downright impossible. Why? Because real writing is messy. A first draft is like a strawberry plant sending out tendrils searching a dozen different directions at once when what the writer really wants is a finely crafted bonsai tree. We teachers have tried to help our students with this over the years, but it is time to admit that we created a problem along the way.

The problem arose from good intentions, though. Teachers are caring. We want to help our students. We want them to be smarter, better, faster, so we give them study tips, mnemonics, and formulas to help them learn. But in trying to simplify the writing process for students, teachers taught the strict structure of the five-paragraph essay. While the five-paragraph form has its benefits and has become pervasive, it isn't *real*. When we challenge our students to find a five-paragraph essay "in the wild," they cannot. Neither can you. They don't exist, at least not in the strictly formulaic way they are so often taught. Writing is too messy to fit such a constrained format in the real world.

Why, then, teach it to students? We contend that the five-paragraph essay's longevity is partly due to assessment needs and the fact that it doesn't take long to write one. It persists because so many in the system want it to, even though it doesn't give students time to work through the complicated stages of writing to arrive at something *good*. If real writing is messy, how can teachers assess it?

The five-paragraph structure gives assessors a nail to hang their hat on. It gives them a structure around which to build a rubric. It gives them something to which points can be assigned. It gives them a language and framework for quickly explaining a B versus an A. It gives testing companies a feasible means of scoring first-draft, time-constrained student writing quickly. But if teachers are supposedly preparing students for "the real world," and if this old school-only essay doesn't exist in the real world, why bother with it at all?

Let's take a step back. Why did Michel de Montaigne develop the essay in the first place some four hundred years ago? He was trying to convey his thinking to a wider audience—thus the verb *essay* that meant "to try or attempt" is now a noun that means "short composition on a single subject." Why write an essay? There are as many answers as there are thoughts in a person's head, but one important reason is that writing is thinking made visible. The act of putting our thoughts down on paper and screen helps us form and clarify our thoughts. It helps us realize when we're wrong and when we're right and, perhaps more importantly, *why* we're wrong or right. Writing an essay allows us to convey these thoughts to others clearly and concisely.

DEFINING THE ESSAY

So what exactly is an old school essay? If you look at that original, broad definition of an essay, an essay could be almost anything. It need only be short and on a single subject. Essays in our general society run the gamut. A single issue of *The New Yorker*, for example, may have a Jelani Cobb political essay, a David Sedaris personal essay, an Elizabeth Kolbert analytical essay, an Ian Frazier travel essay, and a Malcolm Gladwell argumentative essay. (Granted, even by *The New Yorker*'s standards, that would be an all-star issue.) But this has not been the case in schools over the past century.

Schools have, in general, limited the essay by mode and structure. This is a problem because essays can vary widely by mode, especially as more technological tools become cheaper and more available. One essay may be presented in straight alphabetic text, another as a documentary, and a third could be something entirely different. But the essay as a form also serves many purposes. Essays can be argument, exploration, analysis, art, personal reflection—the list could go on. Basically, if words can do it, essays can do it.

All too often, however, essays in school have been five-paragraph formula pieces, and most of those have been literary analysis or simplified arguments about narrow-view topics like school uniforms. For our purposes in this book, the old school essay is an inauthentic academic assignment with imposed structural requirements. Certainly, five-paragraph essays would fall under this category, but so would longer papers that merely expand the same structure to dryly report on symbolism in *To Kill a Mocking-bird* or the cause of the Civil War. This is especially true when the paper's topic is dictated by the teacher.

> Essays can be argument, exploration, analysis, art, personal reflection—the list could go on. Basically, if words can do it, essays can do it.

There is no need to maintain the limits of the old school essay. Essays can be more than five-paragraph formulas. A good one recognizes and struggles with complexity. Essays still exist and still matter; they play a major role in civic literacy, and they need not even be limited to alphabetic text on paper. They also can be about anything. When teachers invite students to write only about literature or simplistic arguments and to do so in only traditional media, we miss opportunities to allow students to explore their world and their own thoughts and beliefs.

Before anyone thinks this book is on a high horse, let us say this text does not exist to cast stones upon composition teachers. The five coauthors of this book have all been guilty of assigning old school essays in one way or another. Most, if not all, writing instructors have at some point. But we can do better, and that is the hope and focus of this book. With practice and a different approach on the teacher's part, our students can learn to use rhetoric fluidly and fluently instead of just filling preset structures and requirements.

It is time—well past time, actually—to move beyond assigning structurally formulaic essays. It is time to invite our students to write real pieces for a real world. Odds are, that seemingly zoned-out student sitting through the lecture about how an essay is like a hamburger is not daydreaming—she is communicating on a global scale via social media. She is constrained by walls only in the literal sense, so there is no need to constrain her essays either.

The notion that teachers are preparing students for the real world they will enter someday is a tired myth. Students *already* live in the real world. Our schools are nestled in the middle of it, so even if the faculty were to successfully insulate the student body, the kids would still make their way through the real world to and from school.

Teachers on Twitter have made this point clearly. Sabra Gerber, a teacher at Fremd High School in Illinois, captured this well when she tweeted, "You're in high school, people ask, 'What do you want to be?' This question sucks. It ignores everything that you already are." A teacher at North Farmington

High School in Michigan, Kevin Ozar, echoed that when he tweeted, "School is the real world for [students]. Saying [that after graduation equals the] real world devalues what kids are feeling and doing in their lives and in class." Our students are already people. They are alive in the real world. It's time our writing assignments honor and reflect that.

To offer our students relevant curriculum, writing instruction must include authentic modes and self-developed topics. Teachers' hearts were in the right place when they began sharing the five-paragraph format with students (and some teachers still use five-paragraph essays, of course). Teachers were trying to help their students, but if that formula ever had a legitimate purpose, its time has passed. Given the technology of the day, our students may already have real-world readers, so we need to help them produce real-world writing.

STUDENTS CAN DO REAL WRITING

But what does real-world writing look like? Therein lies the rub and a big reason for the longevity of the five-paragraph formula. A successful piece of writing changes based on purpose, intended audience, mode of writing, societal context, and more. This is nothing new, of course—Aristotle said this millennia ago. Montaigne understood the varying needs of different pieces of writing, too, when he popularized the essay format some four hundred years ago. Some of his essays are formal arguments on affairs of the state while others are conversational discussions of issues like bad smells. The different purposes and audiences of the writing drove his tone and organization.

Unfortunately, the five-paragraph structure derailed that basic definition of successful writing. A successful five-paragraph essay doesn't care about audience beyond properly applying the formula to earn a grade. Its purpose is a one-dimensional demonstration of material learned in class in hopes of a gold star, but aside from telling jokes on Twitter, gold stars are not the goal of "real" writing.

Authentic writing doesn't get a grade. When we look at essays "in the wild," we judge success very differently. Let's imagine that issue of *The New Yorker* again. A composition teacher may set down the latest Malcolm Gladwell essay and declare, "What marvelous structure!" Everyone else, however, discusses what the essay *said* and the points it made (or didn't make). If a primary goal of an essay is to engage its readers, to get its audience thinking, then the only truly unsuccessful essay is the unread essay, one that faced such serious problems of structure, content, or polish that it led its readers to dump it unfinished. The question for writing teachers is not how to get students to put their thesis at the end of the introduction paragraph. It's how to get students to engage their readers with thoughtful, well-crafted prose.

Our society is amid a renewed push for thoughtful argumentation. In our classrooms, the Common Core State Standards (CCSS) directly call for explicit instruction of argumentative writing. For that reason alone, most of us are revising curriculum, adding nonfiction model texts and argumentative essay assignments. If we keep end goals in mind, though, there is good reason for the CCSS emphasis on argumentation.

Outside our classrooms the call for better argumentation instruction is even stronger. We are at an intriguing point in human history, to say the least. As our ecosystem edges toward potential catastrophe via climate change, much of our political leadership fails to act. In many cases, it ignores the evidence altogether. Some political representatives claim it is not happening or that it is a natural cycle outside of human hands. What we have here is akin to a thesis statement with no essay to back it up. Climate change is only one example—there are hundreds more. Pick a debatable topic, and there is a politician and a talking head on cable news shouting unfounded, simplistic claims about it.

> If a primary goal of an essay is to engage its readers, to get its audience thinking, then the only truly unsuccessful essay is the unread essay, one that faced such serious problems of structure, content, or polish that it led its readers to dump it unfinished.

The 113th Congress (that which served from 2013 to 2015) was widely considered the worst Congress ever for a variety of reasons, but mostly because they did almost nothing (Cillizza 2013). They saw evidence on a range of national and international issues but did not act. This is a failure of, well, many things, but it's also a failure of the thinking built by reading and writing solid arguments. We need better argumentation because we need better thinking. Quite literally for the sake of a functional society and a livable planet, we need to assure that the next generations are better at assessing and analyzing evidence. They need to be better at determining what needs to be done. They need to be better at argumentation, and five-paragraph structure is too limiting to help them wrestle with the complex issues of our day.

THE WIN-WIN

Another area where the old school essay mistakenly caused problems is the omission of complexity. The simplifying of essay structure led to an equating of argumentation and persuasion. They are not the same, and classrooms have too often treated the handling of opposing viewpoints in much the same way as we expect good sportsmanship at an athletic event. A good essay doesn't win at any cost, nor does it give equal merit to opposing viewpoints merely because they're on the other side.

For one thing, there are almost no debates in contemporary society that can or should be posed as "right" or "wrong" choices. Life is more complex than that. Yet, many writing prompts only send students on a quest to prove a correct answer to a question. Is their writing ineffective if it fails to bring everyone to their way of thinking? Not necessarily. Argumentation is not merely a matter of "winning," like it is in persuasion.

A good analogy lies in our own instruction. Student writing is often evaluated for word choice. Papers are revised when a word isn't powerful enough, is overused, or has an improper connotation. This revision should help readers make better sense of the writing. Teachers need to consider word choice too, not just in how to write an effective argument but also why students need to write an effective argument.

The label "argumentative writing" is often interchangeable with "persuasive writing," but it should not be. When someone is referred to as persuasive, the connotation rarely refers to his ability to craft sound arguments. Instead, it brings to mind words like cunning, charming, and anything else associated with the stereotype of a used car salesman. So why associate that negative connotation with debates and arguments, a much-needed (and increasingly missing) part of a civilized society? When students are instructed to engage in an argument, they should know that the goal is not to win. Argumentation is about progress, not being right or winning.

An argument is an opportunity to develop one of the most humble qualities of mankind: the ability to acknowledge we are wrong. Whereas persuasion might just lead students to produce a piece of writing based on preconceptions, argumentation requires students (and teachers) to consider a range of sources, viewpoints, and research. Perhaps most importantly, argumentation also asks students to consider the logic behind the research and viewpoints, which can help students see when they are right or wrong.

When we persuade, we ignore the information that contradicts our position, and we hope that our opponents fail to see it. But when we argue, we open ourselves to new information that may change our views. When students walk away from an argument with a better understanding of how they feel on a topic, even if it differs from the viewpoint they entered the argument with, they accomplish something. It is a win–win. The argument moves forward to more nuanced issues or completely different issues and everyone moves with them together. This is more complex than the persuasive writing that has dominated the classroom. Yes, it's harder, but the payoffs are also bigger.

IF NOT A FIVE-PARAGRAPH ESSAY, THEN WHAT?

Lest it seem like we're still wantonly trashing the five-paragraph essay, let's acknowledge that it can serve a purpose. The formulaic structure is like the training wheels on a four-year-old's bike. But when that child learns to balance and turn, we remove the training wheels. So it goes with essay structure. Essays have a beginning, a middle, and an end. They have a central claim. But from there an essay can go in different directions. In a sense, the old school essay has mostly asked students to merely pedal the bike forward from point A to point B, and the training wheels helped the kids do that. That's not bad, but if we are to go beyond the old school essay, we must remove the training wheels and let the students try out some of the same techniques used by published essayists.

Students understand this when they are explicitly told and reminded that they can go beyond a simple structure. They embrace the notion that content can dictate structure. In our classrooms, when we tell students to take the training wheels off, they sigh in relief at the possibilities. When we require a formulaic structure at some point in their development as writers, it leaves students wondering if and when they should follow it again. Too often, they assume the answer is always. In reality, it's almost never.

> If we are to go beyond the old school essay, we must remove the training wheels and let the students try out some of the same techniques used by published essayists.

Let's break it down with a look at three examples.

First, we have the five-paragraph, formulaic essay. You know the spiel: The introduction is like an inverted triangle (see Figure I.1). It starts broad, and then narrows to the thesis statement which comes as the last sentence of the introduction paragraph. It is like the top bun of a hamburger. The three body paragraphs come next and are all the same in structure. They start with a topic sentence and provide examples before ending with a transition. The conclusion is like a triangle resting on its base: restate the thesis and broaden to a big statement at the end. Regardless of the topic, regardless of the reader, regardless of the context in which it is written, the writer follows this structure.

Before we look at a contemporary example of real-world writing, let's go back to the essay's birth and look at a piece by Michel de Montaigne (1580). "Of a Monstrous Child" is a great text to use with students because it is about the same length as most of their essays. It does not, however, follow a five-paragraph formula (Figure I.1). At six paragraphs long, it looks similar. It has all the same parts—the components are easily recognizable to someone trained in the five-paragraph essay—but a quick structural analysis shows that it is organized in a way that better meets Montaigne's purpose.

He starts with a story that is two paragraphs long and more than half of the essay by word count. There is no thesis statement, no inverted triangle. Instead, he goes into detail recounting the time he saw a conjoined twin's caretakers charging money to let passersby look at the child.

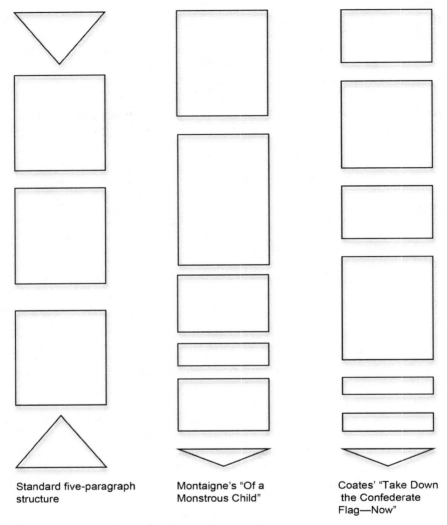

Standard five-paragraph
structure

Montaigne's "Of a
Monstrous Child"

Coates' "Take Down
the Confederate
Flag—Now"

Figure I.1   A comparison of essay structures

He moves on to compare the situation to politics, and then he provides
another example in the shepherd of Medoc. Four paragraphs and 75 percent
of the way into the essay, there is still no thesis statement or "hamburger"
structure.

Finally, Montaigne hits us with the claim at the end. The last two paragraphs clarify the moral point in sharing the anecdotes of the child and the
shepherd. If we had to assign a shape to the essay, it might be a spike. Or
the entire thing might be one huge inverted triangle, but surely the essay is

more filling than eating one bun of a hamburger. In Mitch's classroom, this essay is a perennial favorite. Nobody raises a hand to ask why the thesis isn't in the first paragraph, but *lots* of students raise hands to clarify what exactly he means when he says the shepherd without genitals "has desire, and seeks contact with women."

Montaigne had a clear purpose of passing on a moral virtue to his readers, and he structured the piece accordingly. At the birth of the essay, Montaigne understood that good writing draws in the reader. It puts the content and quality of thought before concerns about structure. If the thinking is good and if the writing is intriguing, the reader will follow along until the point is made at the end.

It is unsurprising that contemporary essays look more like Montaigne's 400-year-old work than a five-paragraph formula. As we wrote the first draft of this book, a racist gunman had just murdered nine worshippers at Emanuel African Methodist Episcopal Church in Charleston, South Carolina. Instantly, social media swirled with demands that the state stop flying the Confederate flag, and Ta-Nehisi Coates' (2015) essay "Take Down the Confederate Flag—Now" appeared the next day.

This is a clear example of Aristotle's point: context demands how a piece be crafted. The citizenry was making demands of the state legislature to remove the flag. The purpose and audience was clear. So, Coates began the essay by establishing that context and explaining the connection between the shooter and the flag. This bears similarity to the inverted triangle introduction because it clearly sets up the essay's topic, but it doesn't end with a thesis statement. The situation is too complex for that, so he must continue into the second paragraph (Figure I.1).

One could contend that buried in the second paragraph lies a thesis statement in "The flag that Roof embraced, which many South Carolinians embrace, does not stand in opposition to this act—it endorses it." A sizable number of Southerners (and some Northerners, too) support the right to fly the Confederate flag, so Coates' statement is certainly debatable.

Coates proceeds to provide more detail and more examples to develop his argument. Similar to Montaigne, he reserves the call to action until the very end when he closes the essay with ten (ten!) imperative simple sentences in a row.

There are surely various ways to interpret Coates' structure. When he quotes the entirety of John Wilkes Booth's letter, is it all part of the same paragraph, or does it count as three paragraphs? Regardless, if a teacher presents it at its shortest form and considers the extended quotes and the commentary that follows each as parts of the same paragraph, respectively, then it is at minimum a seven-paragraph essay. The number of paragraphs is hardly the point, though, because a quick skim of the shapes in the diagrams

shows variety of paragraph length, and therein lies a good deal of the rhetorical impact.

Ignoring differences in development and overall length, a look at only the
structure reveals significant contrasts. The traditional five-paragraph model
lacks variety. It *looks* formulaic. Montaigne and Coates' essays, however,
show different degrees of development for each paragraph based on need and
rhetorical impact. Coates' single-line paragraph near the end, for example, is
extremely powerful *because* it stands alone. The same is true of Montaigne's
final paragraph.

This is not to say all students should start concluding essays with one- or
two-sentence paragraphs. Rather, it sends the message that developing each
paragraph with the same structure is inauthentic and most likely rhetorically
less effective.

It is clear, then, that Coates' piece is no five-paragraph essay, but few would
deem it unsuccessful. It was shared far and wide. It instantly amplified a
movement (Wallace-Wells 2015), and a few days later the governor herself—
a former defender of the flag—publicly called for its removal. Coates' piece
certainly didn't accomplish that on its own, but it added clarity and a center-
piece to a movement. It stands as a fine example of the power of a thought-
fully crafted argumentative essay to make change in our society.

RESPONSIVE INSTRUCTION

This book asks us to move beyond the old school essay, and along the way, we
will focus largely on argumentation itself because that is the route to addressing some of the biggest questions facing composition teachers: How do we
teach students to think? To be honest about the complexity of the issues facing
themselves and their worlds? To form well-constructed arguments? To learn
from good models? To argue in a wide range of writing modes and contexts?

Argumentation has taken on a much larger role in literacy instruction due
to the CCSS, to a renewed push toward project-based classroom work, and
to a growing emphasis on connected learning (Ito 2013). High-quality persuasive writing requires more nuanced rhetoric than a five-paragraph essay,
but it goes beyond just formulaic essays. We are living and teaching in an
era of standardized testing. With ever more focus on the tests, we see more
standardized curricula as well. It comes as no surprise to teachers working in
such contexts, but when we value standards before students (as happens so
often today), our students produce standard, flavorless work.

There is no need for essays and arguments in English to be overly basic,
joyless affairs, though, so how can we help students engage in real, complicated work? That is the true question of this book. Yes, we're moving beyond

the old school essay and are taking the training wheels off our students' "bikes," but what are we doing instead? How can we help our students engage in authentic, constructive work? What does that look like in reading instruction? In writing assignments? In essays or in creative writing?

Surely, there are more questions than answers, but this book will start the conversations and suggest some possibilities. There are five authors of this book, and if five heads are better than one, six or more is better yet. You will have incredible ideas, adaptations, connections, and continuations too. This book is not meant to be an end stop; we hope the work continues in your classrooms too. Instruction can and should change as we learn more about literacy development, new literacies, and new technological tools.

> There is no need for essays and arguments in English to be overly basic, joyless affairs, though, so how can we help students engage in real, complicated work? That is the true question of this book.

We are here to help our students, and that drives every idea in this book. Yes, every activity suggested in the following chapters will undoubtedly address multiple standards, but we'll be honest with you: We didn't develop a single one of these lessons in response to a standard. We made them in response to students' needs. We made them based on our years of experience and learning what works and what doesn't in the classroom.

The old school essay too often put the task before the student. If a task doesn't benefit the students enough, though, we should stop doing it and try something new. Most of the activities in this book are new lessons developed or adapted within the past few years. Our students will only become more adept thinkers if we invite them to help us troubleshoot new activities and fix problems that arise. We can honor our students' real lives in the real world by co-constructing curriculum with them as we all read and write essays, alive in our worlds right now.

So, let's get to the real work.

MODERNIZE THE OLD SCHOOL ESSAY WITH US: CHAPTER OVERVIEWS

Good writing begins with good reading, so chapter 1 looks at the role of reading model texts. We know that students gain vocabulary and syntactic fluency from reading, but what happens if our students read only old essays and excerpts? We are living in a heyday of the written word. It's a safe bet that this very morning, something controversial happened in politics, sports, or entertainment. By lunchtime, there will be a hundred "hot take" essays posted around the web. We can act as guides to help our students find the better essayists out there, and we can invite our students to read their works and model their own writing after them.

Chapter 2 delves into complexity. One of the biggest problems with the old school essay is that it doesn't leave enough room to embrace the complicated nature of an argument. If it's worth arguing about, it will most likely take more than three standardized body paragraphs to explain. True thinking or grappling with hard topics revolves around questions not answers. Good thinking doesn't happen when a writing prompt asks the students to just pick and defend one side for the duration of five paragraphs, so how can we help students understand and explore the complexity of an issue?

As mentioned earlier, the demand for good analysis and argumentation is higher than ever, and chapter 3 focuses on engaging students in civic conversations and giving them opportunities for their writing to *do* something. We highlight various approaches to inviting students to write for social justice and civic engagement, including collaborating with educational partners. Students already write online, but we can help them use online writing spaces like Twitter and comments sections to engage in important civic discourse as well. Among others, we highlight one such collaboration between National Writing Project teachers and KQED, a Bay-Area media outlet that invites students to actively discuss and debate contemporary civic issues.

Perhaps the most common manner in which our students (and teachers) get information isn't even the written word, though. Chapter 4 moves into multimodal texts and different types of arguments. Advertisements are by nature arguments, but how does the camera angle or music choice skew the audience's response? This chapter will dig deeper into how we can help students analyze the arguments presented in multimodal texts and the assumptions they make (and reinforce) about our culture.

Chapter 5 revisits the notion that argumentative writing takes many forms. Though this book focuses mostly on essays, genre is fluid. An essay can be a story, and a story can argue. How can a short story change a reader's mind? Why does *The Lorax* (1971) get more people to consider the environmental impacts of materialism than a president's speech? This chapter will focus on how students can persuade an audience with fiction, creative nonfiction, and poetry, among other genres, just as much as they can with an essay.

Chapter 6 reminds us that we need not reinvent the wheel. Teachers can invite students into new, authentic writing experiences while also maintaining what already works in the classroom. How can teachers adjust what's already there to allow for relevant writing and authentic assessment?

EMBRACING LITERACY IN OUR WORLD: CREATING AN ENGAGING CURRICULUM

Once we step out of the textbook, once we set aside the anthology, once we look through the window or computer screen, we see that literacy skills are crucial to life today. Our grandparents' generation could make it with an eighth-grade education (if that), but that is not the case now. To even understand a current political debate requires a canny reading of a wide range of sources. If we are to help our students navigate and—more importantly—participate in the "real world," all we need to do is bring the world into the classroom. Certainly, our students still benefit from classics, but they also need contemporary works and topics.

The curricular work that lies before us may be daunting, but it is also fun. We are teaching amid a shift. Imagine tutoring new scribes as Gutenberg introduced the printing press. Writing was no longer just copying. Our students need a savvier set of skills than their grandparents did, but in many places, schools are still using the grandparents' curriculum. Let's change that. This work is developing. This work is challenging. This work is exciting. And just like we want for our students, this work is authentic and real. That's why it matters.

Chapter 1

The Living Essay

Reading Contemporary Essays

I realized too late I had done it again. Monday and Tuesday, we read and responded to Orwell's "Shooting an Elephant." Wednesday and Thursday, we read and responded to Swift's "A Modest Proposal." Friday and Monday, we read and responded to Thoreau's "Civil Disobedience." Each time, we read, discussed, analyzed rhetorical decisions, and wrote our own opinions in response.

In and of itself, each of those activities was effective and valuable, but in a row? My students' eyes were beyond glazed over—they had crossed over to lifeless. My lesson plans had turned them into zombies.

I meant well, but life happens. We get busy. Maybe our car breaks down or the team we coach makes the playoffs. There are any number of reasons why teachers fall behind. In my case, we had a baby at home who still needed a middle of the night bottle, so Carrie and I were getting too little sleep. I was just low on time and didn't realize my bad teaching until I looked out at my audience.

When I saw myself reflected in their stares, I had caught myself in the act. I was guilty of delivering a lousy stretch of lessons. Something had to change, so that day at lunch, I paused. I forgave myself for being tired and doing B-level work, then set to making it better. I knew that improving my instruction need not be difficult. My class had been too repetitive, but people don't even notice repetition if the work is engaging. No, the bigger problem with my stale lessons was that we were only studying museum pieces from an anthology. My students needed to read new work too, to see that essays happen "in the wild," so to speak, and not just in textbooks.

I've long invited students to choose their own contemporary novels for independent reading to complement the classics required by the curriculum.

Why wasn't I doing that now with essays? We know that when students are allowed to choose their own texts to read, interest, engagement, and performance all improve. I needed to combine these best practices and let students choose their own contemporary essays to read.

My lunch period that day might have saved my term with those students. The light bulb (finally) went on in my head—if student choice and texts by living authors matter in fiction, they also matter in nonfiction. Students needed to choose some contemporary essays on their own.

—Mitch

The essay is alive.

All too often, it seems students and teachers forget that. Odds are, if a class is reading essays at all, the essays are old. Probably very, very famous—and deservedly so—but old. An essay anthology's table of contents reads like an all-star lineup: Plato. Montaigne. Bacon. Swift. Jefferson. Emerson. Thoreau. Orwell. King. Yes, this is a brilliant batting order, but these writers—and most others included in an essay anthology or textbook—are dead. The average anthology has a handful of contemporary essays at most.

The classic, old essays are certainly worth teaching still in the twenty-first century, but students' reading and writing skills will improve if we add more contemporary essays to their reading. We already know that students lose a love of reading when they read only from textbooks. This happened first with fiction instruction. When publishers gathered the most famous short stories and novel excerpts together in textbooks, the end result was by and large the accidental killing of literary joy for most students. (Not to mention that the textbooks in many classrooms were published decades before the students were even born.) The future English majors might have loved reading four pages of *The Scarlet Letter*, but millions of other Americans did not. More importantly, they didn't gain fluency and literacy skills they could transfer to reading what they *did* want or need to read.

Students won't have textbooks when they're no longer students, and since we want them to be lifelong readers, they can't be dependent on textbooks to choose the good writers for them.

This is not to say textbooks are worthless. In fact, they have come a long way in regards to including newer authors and contemporary authors of color. Textbook companies are now also offering online companion libraries for texts, which allow for more choice. That said, students won't have textbooks when they're no longer students, and since we want them to be lifelong readers, they can't be dependent on textbooks to choose the good writers for them. Plus, when the CCSS suggested a 70/30 nonfiction to fiction split across the school day, they gave educators an opportunity to revisit the textbook approach.

As English departments, especially, revise their curricula to add nonfiction (and hopefully other departments beef up literacy instruction too), an opportunity presents itself. There are great benefits to adding good, new nonfiction to the English curriculum. Also, teachers can change the nonfiction selections their classes already read to include more contemporary readings instead of just old museum pieces. As teachers add nonfiction texts, they have a chance to not repeat the same accidental killing of the joy of reading that happened for so many students with literature textbooks.

In short, we need less textbook and more current texts. The essay as a mode is not dead, and by giving students contemporary essays, teachers can help students become readers, not just demonstrate reading comprehension. If classrooms across America merely add nonfiction by buying stale nonfiction anthologies, the opportunity to improve instruction will be lost. We will have merely replicated an old approach that we already know isn't good enough. Instead, we can use this curricular sea change as a chance to enliven students' reading by both allowing them choice in texts and exposing them to contemporary nonfiction.

To be clear, a nonfiction anthology in and of itself is not a problem, but as mentioned before, students need exposure to essays "in the wild" for a variety of reasons. Students won't always have textbooks, of course, but there's also the fact that textbooks can never have the essays that appear in the moment of a national debate. Students need to learn where to find essays and to see the conversations surrounding them. They need to see the essay in action today, to see the discussion in online comments sections (the thoughtful ones, at least) and the social media dissemination of active, engaged citizens. Students need to learn to support and develop their own learning and learning networks. If our political future is to improve and become thoughtful, we must engage students in choice reading of current essays.

Mind you, teachers need not cut fiction to do all of this. Chapter 5 delves into ways teachers can use fiction in connection to essays and argumentative writing. However, teachers can also take advantage of the CCSS's nonfiction suggestion to add fresh nonfiction pieces that will help students.

WE WRITE WHAT WE READ: A CALL FOR FRESH MENTOR TEXTS

For students as writers, a deeper study of the essay form gives them models. The importance of this cannot be overstated. We learn by watching masters and then practicing those same moves ourselves (Marchetti and O'Dell 2015). This is true of LeBron James growing up watching Michael Jordan. This is true of the hordes of kids viewing Minecraft or other video game tutorials on

YouTube. This is true of current pop stars who watched Michael Jackson's dancing in the eighties. This is also true of essayists.

School has asked students to write essays over the years without often asking the kids to read some first to see how they work. The result is unsurprising. In circumstances like that, students tend to write stale, unoriginal essays that meet an expected—usually five-paragraph—formula. If students are asked to perform in a genre they have little personal experience with as readers, then of course they will need formulas. Teachers can prevent this if they help students see that the essay genre is alive and well in the twenty-first century. Students won't need to rely on formulas if they are exposed to good contemporary essays instead.

So how are students supposed to know a great contemporary essayist when they see one? In this, the teachers can act as a guide. For example, when Dan presents a new author to his class, his first goal is to win over the class with the power of the piece; however, he also stresses that the author is not just a one-hit wonder. As English teachers, we know the better writers of today because it is the world we live in.

Dan shows the students where these authors fit in their world, as well. Contemporary authors interact with society—they are not just delivered to the classroom through a direct pipeline. The students are challenged to find these new names and match them with faces and public personas. Do they have a verified Twitter feed or other social media presence? Has their work been published by reputable magazines, websites, or newspapers? Have they appeared on any number of talk shows from The Today Show to The Tonight Show? Dan's students see that these authors are already recognized by others. It adds legitimacy to their appearance in the classroom, and it often creates a more engaging relationship as students can expect to hear more from these new literary celebrities in the future.

If students are given only anthologized essays to read, teachers risk implying that the essay is a dead, historical medium with no impact on students' lives outside of jumping through academic hoops. Students need to learn from living writers if for no other reason than because people write how they read. If Emerson turned in "Self-Reliance" (1841) today, the instructor might return it marked "Great ideas, but work on concision." Why? It's a classic for a reason, right? Yes, but times change, and language evolves. Students will more effectively use the diction and syntax of the twenty-first century if they read good twenty-first-century writers.

Again, that starts with the readings. Students need model texts. *Everyone* needs model texts. It's how we learn. For most people, the last time they had to write a business letter they did not close their eyes and access their memory banks from seventh-grade English class when they first learned the business letter genre. No, they searched online for a reminder of how business letters are formatted. They found an example and modeled their own writing after it. The natural process is to form a new creative effort on the shoulders of the giants who have come before. Part of a writing teacher's job is to introduce students to the giants, not the gnats, so that they have good models to learn from. Students need to read good essays so that they can write good essays of their own.

Clearly then, students will gain skills by reading classic essayists like Orwell and Emerson. The point here is not to stop introducing students to the essays by the greats, but to invite them to read more and to explore contemporary texts on current ideas and issues. They will not gain enough if the classics are all they read. Times change, and so do writing styles, structures, and expectations. Therefore, students and teachers need to read beyond the essay anthology.

Even the newest essay in a textbook is, by the very nature of compiling and printing a book, not new. Most of the time, a successful essay connects with its audience because its topic is a current, pressing matter. When Montaigne popularized the form, he was trying to share his thoughts with a wider audience than he could by merely speaking his words. Given the ease of publishing online, this advantage of the essay is truer than ever. The advent of the Internet also means that this process moves faster than ever. Now, an essay can be written only moments after an incident and spur change by the following day. As the introduction mentions, Ta-Nehisi Coates' essay about the Confederate flag was met by immediate response and reaction. By reading contemporary essayists, students can see the power of the essay to change minds and even, in fact, change the world.

THE NEW UBIQUITY OF ESSAYS: BOTH EXCITING AND TROUBLING

No political or athletic event happens without a slew of "hot takes" published online almost instantly. Sure, many of these lack in quality, but not all of them. Many of them are excellent essays written quickly to strike while the iron is hot. One major purpose of an essay is to influence thought. Sure, essays may entertain, but really, even with a seemingly silly topic like Montaigne's "Of Smells"—wherein he contends that the best smell is no smell at all—essays are trying to change the reader's mind. If the reader happens to already agree with the essay's claim, then the essay tries to further cement that reader's stance. Why? Essays aim to enact change. This is an important reason to expose students to new essays. They need to see that essays are a vital part of our culture.

An essay aims to take a reader's mind and introduce it to a claim with evidence and reasoning enough to leave that mind in a different shape when

The grocery list implies a claim, but a good essay clearly defines, explains, and supports the claim.

the essay is over. Even a grocery list is an argument. Every written communication is trying to sway its reader in one way or another. That grocery list with chicken on it contends that chicken belongs in the refrigerator. A vegetarian might disagree. Essays, then, take that argumentative nature of writing a step further by including the explication and logical defense of the argument (Toulmin 1958; Hillocks 2011; Smith, Wilhelm, and Fredrickson 2012). The grocery list implies a claim, but a good essay clearly defines, explains, and supports the claim.

This purpose of an essay is not new. What *is* new is that society is now inundated with essays. With the ease and rapidity of publishing, one could say we are living in an essay boom time because opinionated nonfiction appears in just about every textual environment now. The op-ed page of the newspaper has always had essays, but now the form also dominates the landscapes of magazines, the Internet, and even television. A reader can't surf the Internet without running into dozens of essays.

It's fun to ask students if they have ever read an essay outside of school. Most answer *no* because they think of essays only in terms of a five-paragraph, academic exercise. It's fun to watch the baffled looks on students' faces when a teacher pulls up almost any website, from ESPN to Huffington Post to Yahoo, and points to several essays linked from the main page. Essays are everywhere not only because everything is debatable and everyone has a stance, but also because almost anyone can publish their writing now. Regardless of where the reader finds an essay, though, the intent of that writing is clear: Whether the author uses classic argumentation strategies or just hopes to get readers thinking, the end result is that the essay aims to enact *change*.

This omnipresence of essays is exciting but also very challenging and even troubling. Because the culture is drenched with opinion writing, it can be hard to sift the wheat from the chaff. Reading essays well requires the audience to make one critical, nuanced inference after another. This gives all the more reason to invite students to read contemporary essays and to enter the conversations happening in adult society. Those conversations happen all around us whether we want them to or not, and teachers can help students engage in them with greater skill and thought.

A person can't check Facebook to see how her baby niece is doing without also seeing links to essays that demonstrate meager thinking and logical fallacies. Society is inundated with specious logic and agenda-driven weak writing, so the odds are high that we won't end up with a better-informed populace unless teachers help students read and think critically. Without clear teaching of good essays, the end result may be citizens wholly capable of shouting their favorite claims but unable to discern which arguments are accurate and supported.

Living in a world barraged by essays is a blessing and a curse, but in this messy landscape of written words, a teacher can help students identify quality writing. Ideally, after engaging them with well-written essays, students will spot the various hoaxes, logical fallacies, and plain falsehoods that pass as opinion writing, and they will be able to prevent such nonsense from spreading throughout our culture.

But students are less likely to learn how to evaluate the quality and logic of an essay if they read only classic essays. When reading anthologized pieces, students tend to hunt for big ideas to use when discussing, responding to questions, or taking a quiz. Students don't, however, *engage*. With contemporary texts about important topics of our day, they can learn to discern good writing from bad, *and* they can enter the pressing debates themselves. They don't need to wait until they're in "the real world." Students must join the current conversations, and teachers need to help students read a lot of high-quality essays, both new and old, so that students can hone their critical thinking, reading, and writing abilities.

> Students must join the current conversations, and teachers need to help students read a lot of high-quality essays, both new and old, so that students can hone their critical thinking, reading, and writing abilities.

CHOICE IN READING

That all sounds nice, but it's daunting. One upside to a textbook is that the teacher already knows that the material inside has been deemed worthy. But working with only anthologies means missing a boatload of opportunities to help students see the relevancy of essay writing.

As the introduction to this book mentions, students already live in the real world, and a good curriculum lets students engage in real-world work. Reading fresh essays is one way to do that. Inviting students to write in response to them is even better, and students writing to their own concerns and desires for change is best. To reach that point, though, it helps to start with good readings, and to truly achieve relevancy for students, students must have choice.

The research is clear: Students are more motivated and do better work when they are allowed to choose their own readings. A number of master teachers have written on the benefits of letting students choose their own books (Atwell 1998; Beers 2002; Kittle 2012; Krashen 2004), and their studies show that choice leads to increases in student reading. Penny Kittle has seen former nonreaders churn through forty books in a year (Kittle 2012). Many teachers who have moved to choice reading have similar stories. While much of the research done on choice reading has focused on novels, students respond equally well when offered choice in nonfiction reading.

A quick Internet search for high school reading lists shows nonfiction books are an increasing presence on choice lists. The authors of this book have all seen students choose narrative nonfiction like *Moneyball, Fun Home, A Long Way Gone,* and *The Glass Castle* and engaging argumentative texts like *Fast Food Nation, Overachievers,* or *Outliers* when allowed to do so. Students will benefit from choice in reading individual essays too; plus, this will also pay off in students' own writing. When students read choice novels in Mitch's classes, they gain the same benefits Beers, Kittle, Atwell, and others have written about. When given choice, students often report finishing a book for the first time in years (and sometimes, for the first time *ever*). That same success could happen with essays if students have choice for reading contemporary essays.

LIFELONG READERS

Most literacy teachers dream of helping students become lifelong readers. Most also dream of students being active and engaged citizens as adults. What does that look like? What is the long-term goal for nonfiction reading? Reading for enjoyment *and* enlightenment. Reading for information *and* insight. Reading widely *and* deeply. If that's the long-term goal, and since students are already living in the real world, then why not ask them to start reading like that now?

The trick is introducing students to the sources of well-crafted, intelligent essays—preferably to the sources frequented by engaged lifelong readers—and inviting students into those literate conversations. It's safe to say that the average teenager doesn't frequent, for example, *The New Yorker*, *The Atlantic*, or the weekend editions of *The Wall Street Journal* and *The New York Times*, but that doesn't mean they can't. Also, once they do open a magazine or website, students aren't going to instantly be drawn to every piece there, but neither are readerly adults.

How many of us, after all, read a given issue of *The New Yorker* from cover to cover? If teachers lead the students to the sources of good writing, though, the students can choose the individual pieces that do appeal to them. When we let them sift through the essays, choose the ones that they are drawn to, and take each other's recommendations—just like how engaged adult readers often choose essays—then they will read.

Of course, a teacher can't merely send students to the Internet and say "read only the good essays." If the teacher puts sensible limits on which sources students should go to, the risk of encountering bad writing can be greatly mitigated. This can accomplish a couple of goals. One, teachers can help students see that essays are alive and well, but two, it can also help students learn to discern good writing from bad outside of textbooks.

After students have had a chance to read some contemporary essays from dependable sources, ask them how this writing compares to what they normally read online. An essay about medical practice by Atul Gawande in *The New Yorker* is bound to lead the reader to deeper thinking than a Buzzfeed list of the "11 most amazing small dog breeds." If we model how lifelong readers assess the merits of one piece of writing compared to another, our students will develop this ability too. It must be a long-term goal for students to be able to identify good writing and good thinking on their own.

The experience of reading essays from proven sources like *The Atlantic* and talking about how those are different from click-bait articles like Buzzfeed lists will help students become savvier judges of unknown sources. Ultimately, students need to evaluate the merit of writing on their own without teachers or textbooks acting as filters. As with any skill, if the students start this process under a mentor's tutelage and continue to practice, they will become masters themselves.

THE ESSAYS INDEPENDENT READING PROJECT

So how might this look in the classroom? Give students guidelines and facilitate, but don't just assign the same essays to all readers. To that end, Mitch developed a choice-reading unit for essays. It received a painfully straightforward name: The Essays Independent Reading Project (EIRP). It's not a flashy title, but at least students know what they should do: read essays on their own. The EIRP could be summed up as "give students good sources of essays and ask them to find and read a bunch," but to assure that students pick up on good rhetorical maneuvers that they can apply in their own writing, it can be helpful to set some parameters.

Find Good Essays

There are dozens of sites that publish good writing, but students often find the best essays at the websites of already-respected publications like *The Atlantic*, *The New York Times*, or *The Wall Street Journal*. This list of websites has repeatedly led Mitch's students to good essays:

- http://www.theatlantic.com/
- http://www.newyorker.com/

- http://www.wsj.com/news/types/the-saturday-essay
- http://opinionator.blogs.nytimes.com/
- http://longreads.com/
- http://aeon.co/magazine/
- http://longform.org/
- http://www.aldaily.com/

Note that several of these sites compile work published elsewhere and will link to original sites (which are often still the old-guard like *Vanity Fair* and *Harper's*). Of course, there are dozens of other sites with excellent writing. (*McSweeney's, The Awl*, and *The Toast* all spring to mind.) By no means does this list contain the only websites a teacher could use to lead students to good essays. As long as the teacher knows the site has high-quality, reputable essayists, it will work.

As with any other assignment, it is helpful to provide some guidelines while still leaving room for student choice. Some students, for example, will need a required number of essays to read. That number depends on how much time is available in the curriculum, but most teachers we know who have used this format set the baseline between five and ten essays. Many students read more because once they discover the wealth of interesting writing, they keep going. While this is the hope for all students, some need a strict requirement to motivate them.

But does the teacher need to have read all of the options students can choose from? The answer should be *no*. For one, that's impossible, but more importantly, students are learning how to select and judge writing on its own merits using their own sensibilities and critical reading skills to determine the quality of the writing. Teachers can and should model this and demonstrate for students how to choose and evaluate an essay.

In several instances, this book refers to the process of finding a contemporary essay as reading an essay "in the wild." This is why giving students a list of usually dependable publications helps. For someone who has not frequented websites like these or who grew up in a household without periodicals, it really can feel like navigating the wild. Teachers can give students the tools they will need, show the students how to use them, and then set them loose to do the work on their own.

Share the Readings

So, finding and reading essays is the obvious first step. This takes time, as students will need to explore the websites and find interesting essays. After students have had time to read at least a few essays, they start to share.

1. Invite students to offer 30-second recommendations. Which essays should fellow students read and why?

2. Ask students to contribute links to the best essays using a common web tool like LiveBinders (http://www.livebinders.com/) or Diigo (https://www.diigo.com/) so that each class can create its own anthology of recommended current essays. Social bookmarking—the sharing of sources with others—is helpful for sharing recommendations to read as well as honing contemporary research skills.

3. In small groups, discuss what made the good essays effective. How did the writers engage the students as readers? What made one essay better than another?

The order of these events is negotiable. It's also helpful to ask students to respond in writing. In most cases, the discussions are better if students have had a chance to write about the essays first, but the flip is true too: Talking first can lead to improved writing. This is ultimately a judgment call for the teacher, and mixing up the order can be best.

Respond in Writing

The teacher can provide students with options for the written responses. Here are a few:

- Make an outline of the piece showing how the author developed the argument. Focus on understanding the piece's logic and structure, and identify the elements of the argument using Toulmin Model terminology (claim, evidence, reasoning, backing, qualifiers, and rebuttals).
- Respond to the claim(s) made in the essay. To what extent and why do you agree or disagree with the essay's argument? In what circumstances might the essay's claim(s) be accurate, and when might it be wrong?
- Conduct a brief rhetorical analysis of the essay. Explain *what* the writer did, *how* the writer did it, and *why* the writer did it.

The intent here is twofold. It helps to let students analyze and respond to contemporary work in the ways they are used to doing with classic essays, so they can see that current writers make similar rhetorical moves. Students also benefit when teachers help them see how the essays can be models for the students' own writing. A primary aim of the EIRP is to help students see that successful writing does not follow the same formula every time and that contemporary essays allow students to examine the traditional "rules" of essays (Campbell 2010).

Outlines Reveal Structure

The mere act of reading several contemporary essays will help students start to see this, but students often just "play school" and do what's asked of them without really thinking about it. This is one reason for providing the three response prompts above. Asking them to make an outline of an essay assures that students break down the structure and notice exactly how the author has avoided a five-paragraph formula (Figure 1.1).

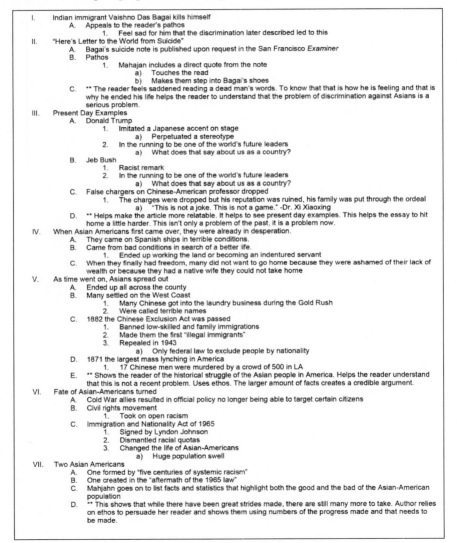

Figure 1.1   Grace's outline of "The Two Asian Americas" by Karan Mahajan, published in *The New Yorker*

A student's outline can also analyze various rhetorical elements used by the author, as Grace did with her outline in Figure 1.1. Here, too, the teacher can guide students by giving them a list of suggested techniques to look for. Among hundreds of possibilities, here are a few. Students can outline the structure and take note of the following:

- the location of (or even existence of) the claim,
- the order of body paragraphs,
- the use of narrative support,
- what kinds of evidence the author cites,
- where the author uses direct quotes, paraphrases, or summaries,
- where the author uses first person or second person, and
- where the author's style is evident, for example, purposeful use of sentence fragments or run-ons, especially short or long paragraphs, use of slang, etc.

Remember to Apply the Techniques

It is important to keep purpose in mind at this point. Asking students to find rhetorical maneuvers should not be a hoop-jumping activity. Remember, the goal here is to improve students' own writing. When asking students to find rhetorical details, ask them to also identify which moves worked on them as readers, and why, so that they can, in turn, practice those same techniques in their own writing.

To narrow the options and make this activity more easily accessible for students, it can help to ask them to analyze only one essay that particularly appealed to them. They can respond to the essay by addressing questions like:

- If you agreed with the essay, why? How did the writer persuade you? Identify one such technique and use it in your response writing.
- How did the essay grab your attention? How did it keep your attention throughout? Identify that rhetorical maneuver and use it in your response writing.
- What specific details or examples does the essay use? Why did these details and examples engage you as a reader? In your response writing, mimic the essay's use of details.
- How did the essay's word choice appeal to you? Was it formal? Informal? How can you adjust your diction choices in your next piece of writing to mimic this effective word choice?
- Find a sentence that you thought was particularly good. Maybe it effectively made a point. Maybe it grabbed your attention in a creative way. Maybe it surprised you. What kind of syntactic structure did it use? In your own writing, try using the same syntax and mirror the structure of that sentence.

- How did the essay appeal to its audience? Who do you think was its target audience? Write a short piece mimicking the essay's rhetorical appeals to a specific audience.

The list could go on, but a handful of guiding questions should be enough to get students trying to apply the writers' techniques in their own work. Once that happens, the students will soon craft much livelier prose of their own. It is worth noting that the students will likely fail along the way as they try new techniques, but that's the natural order of the learning process, of taking risks and trying new approaches. They might stumble as they move away from the standard five-paragraph structure in the same way that young children fall over once the training wheels come off their bikes. With practice, though, the students will write more natural, more interesting essays. It can take time, but it will come.

> It is worth noting that the students will likely fail along the way as they try new techniques, but that's the natural order of the learning process, of taking risks and trying new approaches.

NEXT STEPS

But how can the students get there? What are those next pieces of writing for the students? Another goal of the EIRP is to engage students in current debates, so ask students to respond with their own argumentative writing. For example, the introduction mentions Ta-Nehisi Coates' essay on the lowering of the Confederate flag. A student may choose to read that piece and be struck by his stance and the history of the flag. This is an opportunity for that student to write her own argument on the matter.

In another case, perhaps two friends read and disagreed about Elizabeth Kolbert's essay (2013) wherein she claims that sports should be separated from the high school experience. These students can write opposing essays and maybe even publish them in the student newspaper. Students' writing topics are limited only by the number of arguments in the world, which certainly seem to be limitless.

Even students writing their college entrance essays need models and can find the value in reading models of reflective essays—not just the standard "how to" for college essay books. Dawn's students also read a variety of essays, including narrative essays from the *This I Believe* series and then they use these as models for creative nonfiction or reflective essays. A process like the EIRP can work here too because exposure to real-world essays can help students see that the genre of the "college essay" is more than just a one-hoop wonder.

The EIRP is not intended to be a finite project. Once students have had a chance to explore good sources of current essays, one hopes they will go back for more. Even if they don't, having spent time with good contemporary writing will improve the students' reading and writing. We learn from mentors. We improve by practicing. The EIRP allows students to do both, especially if the classroom is a writer's space, one where students write often and are allowed to try out new techniques and fail without serious consequence. To better prepare students for real, non-formulaic writing, teachers need to help students realize that "real" essays are complex and varied—just like the real world and just like their own, real lives.

IN SHORT

- Students need to read good essays to write better essays of their own.
- To write well in the twenty-first century, students need to read twenty-first-century essays too, not just older pieces in textbooks.
- To ensure that students read good contemporary essays, teachers can provide a list of highly regarded publications and websites.
- Students need to analyze the contemporary essays to make sure they see the structures and techniques being used.
- To improve their writing, students must be encouraged to try those structures and techniques in their own writing, even if taking those risks initially results in struggles with their writing.
- If we want students to be lifelong readers, writers, and thinkers, then we must invite them to participate now in the same activities as reading, writing, thinking adults.

Chapter 2

Exploring the Complex Gray Area

Some of my best teaching moments come out of what appear, initially, like mistakes. They occur when lessons veer off in directions I hadn't intended or anticipated. I discover them in moments that feel, at first, like failures. Like writing, teaching is often as much about discovery as it is recitation of what is already known.

Last year, I designed a short unit that used public service announcements from the New Zealand Transportation Agency as the subjects of rhetorical analysis. As I planned it, my students would watch the PSAs, then analyze them. We would look closely at the visuals, at the implied arguments, at the appeals to pathos, logos, and ethos. We would treat these PSAs, in short, like any other advertisement, or any other piece of visual media open to analysis. (Visual and multimodal arguments are discussed further in chapter 4.)

The PSA "Mistakes" from the New Zealand Transport Agency (2014) shows two cars about to collide, but before they strike, time freezes and the drivers have the opportunity not only to confront one another but also to consider the consequences about to unfold. As my class started the discussion over this PSA, the lesson took an unexpected turn. There were two ways in which the students wanted to look at the PSA that I hadn't anticipated: one involved describing, in great detail, the close calls they had witnessed in automobiles over the course of their own lives; the other arose when a student asked the seemingly simple question, "Whose fault was it?" For a few minutes, the class argued back and forth, taking sides and marshaling evidence. Just before I stepped in to redirect the conversation back toward the original goals for the lesson, another student asked, without a trace of snark, "Who cares?"

Indeed. Who cares?

While it may be possible, in the end, to argue persuasively that driver A or driver B was most at fault, the student was absolutely right: what would be the point of doing so? What makes that PSA so provocative, so effective, and, in the end, so persuasive, is that it doesn't ignore the potential complexity of the situation. It doesn't pretend that the point of the short film is to blame one side or the other. It doesn't pretend that one of the two men is simply guilty, or that the question of guilt is all that matters. It calls on us to reckon with an important, muddled, and potentially devastating situation.

This is true about writing, as well. Truly persuasive writing does not ignore complications. It does not pretend that issues, ideas, and questions are more simplistic than they truly are. If it is to be persuasive, it must move toward complication, embrace and address complication, and demonstrate not only how complex the issue, the situation, or the story at hand really is, but also how that situation might actually be resolved.

Unfortunately, this is rarely how we teach students to write. Instead, we treat "persuasive" or "argumentative" writing as a genre unto itself, one with its own unique rules, and one comprised only of essays written from extreme stances in response to binary prompts. We imply that writing that eschews simplicity and easy answers and instead revels in complexity and ambiguity cannot possibly persuade an audience. We ignore the gray areas where most of us live our beautifully human, beautifully messy, beautifully complex lives.

—Dirk

STANDARDIZED RESPONSES TO STANDARDIZED PROMPTS

As part of standardized end-of-course assessments, many states now ask students to respond to what are often labeled "persuasive writing prompts." We see them, too, on selective secondary school entrance exams and on national aptitude tests like the SAT. These prompts typically ask students to "take a position" on an issue and develop an essay that supports that position.

Here's one the Virginia Department of Education published: "The British naturalist and politician John Lubbock wrote, 'Your character will be what you yourself choose to make it.' Do we choose our own character traits, or is our character formed by influences beyond our control? Take a position on this issue. Support your response with reasons and examples" (2014).

In its form and its assigned task, it's the same kind of prompt we find on standardized test throughout primary and secondary education—prompts such as,

- "Is success more a matter of persistence or ability?"
- "Do we accomplish more if we are always working or does inaction also serve an important purpose?"

- "Is it more important to do work one finds fulfilling or work that pays well?"
- "Do works of art have the power to change people's lives?"
- "Do you agree or disagree that being yourself is the greatest accomplishment in this world?"

Because teachers and students ultimately have to answer to these tests, we often find ourselves in a rush to teach easily repeatable structures. We end up encouraging students to plug their responses into a preexisting formula for a "persuasive essay": an introduction of four to six sentences, probably starting with an extremely generic and implausibly universal hook (such as, "Throughout all of human history, the wisest of our philosophers have wondered why some people achieve success and others do not") and ending with an explicit, extreme thesis statement (like, "It is clear that success is a matter of persistence, not of ability"). Three body paragraphs follow, each one presenting a single piece of evidence or a single specific reason that supposedly supports that thesis. Finally, the conclusion reviews the evidence and restates the thesis in slightly different words.

It's efficient. It's repeatable. But what do students learn when they successfully fill in the blanks in such a formula? What can they take forward and build on?

Have they become better writers? Probably not. Most of them were merely repeating something they already knew how to do.

Have they thought more thoroughly about the topic at hand? Again, probably not. By ignoring the potential complexity of the issue and reducing the topic to something worthy only of a simplistic "yes or no," "one or the other," "this or that" binary question, we've eliminated both the need for and the possibility of thought. Of exploration. Of discovery—which is exactly what writing often is and arguably what education should be.

Perhaps most damning is that students find it nearly impossible to genuinely care about what they're writing when asked to respond formulaically to a prompt like "Is success more a matter of persistence or ability?" They can feign interest long enough to choose a side to argue, but can generate no enthusiasm beyond that. Often, students even make that choice arbitrarily or consider only what they suspect will be easiest to argue instead of what they actually believe. As H. L. Mencken (1982) wrote, the main thing most children learn in school is how to lie. Anne Whitney calls this acting "schoolish" (2011). In other words, they learn to pretend to care, incredibly briefly, about something they're forced to do.

EXPLORATORY CONVERSATIONS

Fortunately, there is potential for greater student engagement in the process of learning to write on demand as authentic writing opportunities prepare our students for a variety of writing situations, even for standardized tests. The writing prompts on such tests traditionally ask students to take a position or develop their point of view on an issue. While some offer students a reminder that they can answer in an alternative fashion, most prompts are set up with an implicit or explicit binary choice. And students already know how to "pick a side," or how to "agree or disagree." What they typically need help learning is how to carry a comprehensive argument to an effective conclusion.

Consider the question of whether success is more a matter of persistence than ability. Before Dirk ever showed his students that particular writing prompt, he asked them to brainstorm possible reasons that some people achieve great success while others struggle. The lists they came up with, individually and collectively, were thoughtful, far-ranging, and interesting, and they showcased a willingness to confront the question truthfully and to recognize its potential complexity.

As they discussed their reasons, students spoke of how persistence in the absence of ability is essentially as meaningless as the reverse. They spoke of how often luck is a factor in achievement. They spoke of the importance of having supportive parents or a particularly hard-nosed but caring coach. They spoke of the possible advantages or disadvantages of being born in particular centuries or parts of the world.

One student wondered whether LeBron James would have been at all successful if born in 1794 instead of 1984—obviously, he pointed out, not as a basketball player, in any case. Another student brought up the surprising findings about success in Malcolm Gladwell's *Outliers* (2008). Clearly, they were interested in the issue. They discussed these possibilities passionately, but not a single student tried to argue that one individual reason mattered more than any other. Rather, they demonstrated what Andre Dubus III asserted in a 2012 interview with *Writer's Digest*: "I think the deeper you go into questions, the deeper or more interesting the questions get. And I think that's the job of art."

Two days later, though, when Dirk gave his students the writing prompt in its original form ("Is persistence more important than ability in determining a person's success? Plan and write an essay in which you develop your point of view on this issue."), his students seemed to forget every moment of that active, engaged discussion. Instead of teasing out the complexities and complications of the issue, they wrote simplistic arguments for one side or the other. Instead of grappling honestly and thoroughly with the various factors that might determine a person's success, they lapsed into a formula, chose a side, and pretended to care about it for five paragraphs.

This is not entirely their fault. For too long, whether as a result of increasing standardized testing or not, school has taught students to see questions and issues of potential complexity as what David Rosenwasser and Jill Stephen call "false dichotomies" or "false binaries" (1997). As Mike Miller of Thomas Jefferson High School of Science and Technology pointed out, students sometimes get taught to believe that "take a position on this issue" or "develop your point of view on this issue" means "choose one of two apparent options" (2014). Consequently, when asked to complete such a prompt, Dirk's students fell back on easy, over-generalized, rigid thesis statements and one-sided arguments devoid of complexity, voice, and engagement.

After Dirk had assessed their largely dull essays on persistence and innate ability, he asked them which they enjoyed more: the original discussion or the writing prompt. Every one of them, even those who genuinely like writing, chose the discussion. When asked why, they said that when discussing the issue, they thought about the question more; they weren't required to choose a side; they weren't trying to fit evidence where it didn't really fit; they considered things they hadn't considered before; they thought about themselves more. When writing, they simply asked which side made the most sense to write about in a short amount of time.

When asked if they wanted to write another essay to the same prompt, they said absolutely not. Dirk asked them if they wanted to talk more about what factors might contribute to success and they said sure. Clearly, their interest in the subject hadn't entirely waned, but they could see no way to reconcile their desire to probe the question further with the seeming demands of the writing prompt, a prompt that suggested, to them, that "develop your point of view on this issue" meant "choose a side."

TAKING A POSITION

A month later, Dirk gave students another issue to consider. This time, he asked them to write freely and openly about who they thought they were, about their identities, and about how they had become the people that they were. During a subsequent class, he asked them to write about the kinds of forces that they felt were trying to shape them or change them as people.

During another class, they wrote about the extent to which they felt comfortable being themselves in school or at home or with their friends.

After each writing, they shared their thoughts enthusiastically with one another and with the class. They wondered about what had influenced their personalities and their beliefs. They considered whether the primary forces trying to mold their behavior were more benevolent or self-serving. They asked how much of themselves was truly their own creation and how much was the result of environmental influence. One student declared that she didn't know whether she was being herself around her friends or family because she didn't know what her true self was.

This time, when given the writing prompt, students spent 15 minutes discussing the language of the prompt itself:

> *Author Ralph Waldo Emerson wrote, "To be yourself in a world that is constantly trying to make you something else is the greatest accomplishment." Do you agree or disagree with Emerson's statement about individuality? Take a position on this issue. Support your response with reasons and specific examples.* (Virginia Department of Education 2014)

When asked what "take a position" actually means, students quickly realized that the prompt did not explicitly ask them to choose one polar extreme or the other. "So, my position could be that I'm somewhere in the middle?" a student asked. As a class, we agreed that, in fact, it could be—but that the student also should be wary of coming across as wishy-washy or lacking a position. Her challenge would be to show how her position, wherever on the spectrum between "yes" or "no" it might be, was a valid one. Her challenge would be to explore how "being yourself" might be a far more complicated matter than simply agreeing or disagreeing with Emerson. Perhaps, she might find that "the history of [her] various changes in thinking is, in many ways, the thesis of [her] essay" (Rosenwasser and Stephen 1997).

This time, Dirk's students' essays were far more interesting and far more engaged with the topic. Only a few of them included a formulaic introduction or repetitive conclusion. Instead, students interrogated the prompt itself, asking what it meant "to be yourself," asking to what extent it was good or bad that the world was constantly "trying to make you something else," asking whether it was possible to have a single, individual self.

Dirk could see students discovering what they thought and felt as they were brainstorming, drafting, and revising—even in the limited amount of time they had to write the essay. When offered the opportunity to take their essays home to continue working on them before our next class meeting, about one-fourth of Dirk's students chose to do so, whereas not a single student had done so when responding to the "persistence vs. ability" prompt.

What they had done, of course, was discover the complexity of the issue behind the question. They had moved toward complication instead of pretending that the issue was simplistic or one-sided. They had explored themselves and their world as they grappled with Emerson's statement. They had produced writing far more relevant to the world in which they live every day. In doing so, many of them had written truly persuasive essays.

In addition, their writing was more reflective of the kind of reading we do in our classroom. The novels, plays, and essays that we read and discuss together present us characters, cultures, ideas, and questions that, as different as they are, share one particular trait: they're all relatively complicated. They don't pretend that people, or the world, or ideas, are simple. If they do, we dismiss them as the equivalent of after-school television specials and go looking for something better.

Moreover, the dialogic nature of this work supports student learning and idea development as critical thinkers (Bakhtin 1981; Greene 1978; Juzwik et al. 2013; Stock 1995). Simply establishing a binary that ignores the complexity of the works and ideas studied in class can lead to weaker writing or less engaged students. Even students who know the content find themselves backed into a formulaic box, unable to show the richness of their thinking.

What they had done, of course, was discover the complexity of the issue behind the question. They had moved toward complication instead of pretending that the issue was simplistic or one-sided. They had explored themselves and their world as they grappled with Emerson's statement. They had produced writing far more relevant to the world in which they live every day. In doing so, many of them had written truly persuasive essays.

Like Dirk, Dawn has seen this in her teaching. One student who had developed an extensive research project on bullying struggled when asked about it in a standardized writing prompt. The rhetorical confines of the situation stifled the student's writing (Homan and Reed 2014). When students are forced to fit complicated arguments into an expected preset structure, their writing will suffer.

DIGGING DEEPER FOR WORTHWHILE ARGUMENTS

Now that Dirk's students had wrestled with this complexity, with this gray area, in their own essays, his classes could look much more closely at how published authors do the same thing. They could discuss the ways in which *The Great Gatsby* (1925) refuses to reduce wealth, desire, love, or ambition to simplistic cautionary arguments. Or they could investigate the points at which Neal Stephenson, in the interface culture section of *In the Beginning . . . Was the Command Line* (1999), refuses to issue an easy condemnation of Microsoft Windows and people's dependence on such Graphical User Interfaces.

As they explored professional texts, they considered the structures of those works: how introductions often did not end with extreme, argumentative thesis statements, but instead actually performed the function of *introducing* a given topic or question. We discussed how conclusions could genuinely reflect on the material within a given piece and actively *conclude* something about that material, rather than merely rephrasing what was supposedly the introduction.

Conclusions should genuinely reflect on the material within a given piece and actively *conclude* something about that material, rather than merely rephrasing what was supposedly the introduction.

As we might expect, students sometimes struggled with incorporating these models into their own writing. Some initially flailed a bit when set free from the formulas they were accustomed to following in their essays. Some produced essays more disordered than persuasive. Now that students were more engaged with the material, however, students were much more willing to actively revise their papers and to look for organic and personally meaningful ways to bring order to their thoughts.

What Dirk's students came to want, and what they demanded of the standardized prompts in his classroom, was the opportunity to learn. They wanted to consider the ideas put in front of them honestly and thoroughly, not to simply plug words into a formula to demonstrate that they had mastered that formula. Instead of writing essays that simply argued whether or not Jay Gatsby is a tragic hero, they asked what might make him tragic, what sorts of myths and illusions he believed in and why, and the extent to which he might be admired for those beliefs. They embraced questions and possibilities that complicated their initial thoughts and did their best to consider those complications.

In Dirk's classroom, one of the ways students begin to respond to an issue, a film, or a work of literature is by completing what they call an "X–Y statement." In such a statement, a student writes, "This work seems to be about X, but is really about Y." They allow themselves to have an initial reaction to the work, but then force themselves to complicate that initial understanding. Often, students will write several such statements before pursuing one further. Here are three examples of students' X–Y responses to *Hamlet*:

- *Hamlet* seems to be about the human need for vengeance, but is really about the impossibility of acting with a clear conscience even when seeking revenge.

- *Hamlet* seems to be about the possibility of self-knowledge, but is really about the lies we tell ourselves in order to explain and justify our decisions and our lives.
- *Hamlet* seems to be about not being able to trust other people, but is really about the acts we put on to get other people to trust us so that we can use them for our own ends.

Once they have completed one or more X–Y statements, students will continue to subject that reading of the work to questions and other possibilities. They do not ignore evidence that complicates their first impressions (Rosenwasser and Stephen 1997). Instead, they consider the work as thoroughly as they can before starting to finalize their understanding of it.

Earlier this year, Dirk's English 11 Honors students worked toward deeper, more complex understandings of books they had individually chosen from a selection of classic and contemporary works. They explored a central idea or argument of the work through a series of three letters, each one responding to an earlier idea by complicating and developing further that previous letter's assertions. With each letter, students had to both acknowledge and deal with complicating evidence, each time allowing their "reading" of the work in question to evolve.

In his first letter, Peter explores several different possibilities for the central "argument" of Max Barry's *Lexicon* (2013), asking at one point, whether "there is a base language, or base 'code' that is ingrained into us as humans, enabling us to communicate or be controlled" (see Figure 2.1). In the second letter (see Figure 2.2), he replies, "The strongest bare word, or base communication, is affection and love. That is the key to what makes humans collectively strongest together."

Do you remember the book you told me to read called Lexicon? It was one of the most captivating books I've read in a long time. The two parallel story lines, in different views of the world at different times, was fresh. It brought some interesting questions up to me after I finished reading. I could not explicitly tell what the book was trying to bring up thematically. Was it the struggle of two individuals against society? As in Emily and Harry struggling with the Poets to survive and the wedge that it inevitably put between them. Or that there is a base language, or base "code" that is ingrained into us as humans, enabling us to communicate or be controlled? Could it even be all about human bonds? The unbreakable love between Emily and Harry?

Figure 2.1 Excerpt from Peter's first letter

That's just the crude summary. What was our friend Max Barry trying to show us? Max made a perplexing puzzle to show us the bond between two people, but also how resilient that bond is. Even after Harry was brainwashed by Emily to forget her, his resilient brain knew his true love even if he did not. An astounding discovery, right? The strongest bare word, or base communication, is affection and love. That is the key that to what makes humans collectively strongest together.

Figure 2.2   Excerpt from Peter's second letter

Love makes us independent. That's weird, right? We normally think about couples in twos, but they are one. They have their single bond, they share a single heart. Love, that single independent relationship, can be applied not only between a couple, but between people and their country. One people united under one flag. People love their countries and feel a central nationalistic pride. They feel as one. Love makes us independent; it makes us into a single being.

Figure 2.3   Excerpt from Peter's third letter

In his third letter (see Figure 2.3), Peter develops that idea further to conclude, first, that "[love] is the highest power of human connectedness" and, finally, "Love makes us independent. That's weird, right? We normally think about couples in two, but they are one. They have their single bond, they share a single heart." An essay about the possibility that love is both a connection and a uniquely unifying force would certainly be a more interesting, more insightful, and more critically thoughtful than one written about what could have been his original thesis.

All of this, of course, might be fine in a classroom. It might be fine when students have several days to work through such complexity and to discuss, as thoroughly as they can, the potentially interesting questions at the heart of the essay prompts they're likely to see on future tests. But what can they do on those tests themselves? Can they use what they've learned about engaging themselves with the gray, messy in-betweens of their lives and our world and succeed on a standardized test?

They can.

TEST RUBRICS DON'T PRECLUDE REAL WRITING

Virginia's Department of Education lists these as the qualities of a "superior" essay on the End-of-Course (11th grade) state writing test (2011):

- Focuses on a clear position and adapts content to purpose, audience, and tone
- Draws effective conclusions
- Addresses counterclaims when relevant
- Contains precise and relevant evidence
- Organizes ideas in a sustained and logical manner
- Develops a rhythmic flow
- Contains highly specific word choice

Nowhere in that list is there a suggestion that students must take an extreme stance on the issue given in the prompt. Instead, they must "focus on a clear position," even, in theory, one somewhere in between the two opposed false binaries. Of course, students must still have a position. Their responses cannot be wishy-washy, neutral, or undecided, but they can be nuanced, complex, and sophisticated.

Likewise, while the five-paragraph essay formula may lend itself to a simplistic structure built on an extremely one-sided thesis plus three pieces of supporting evidence, the rubric does not claim such a structure is necessary. Instead, students must organize their ideas in a "sustained and logical manner" and connect their ideas "within and across paragraphs" through the use of "highly effective and purposeful transitions." Yes, exploring how an issue might be more complicated than it initially seems can lead to organizational challenges for students as they write, but students more invested in the questions within the prompt tend to be more invested in finding ways to present their thoughts clearly. Delving into complications will lead to a better essay—especially if students have, in class, read a wide variety of real-world essays and used them as models for their own writing.

A superior essay "draws effective conclusions." This is where thoughtful, thorough exploration of a presented topic can truly shine. In a five-paragraph essay, the introduction is really a conclusion. Students generate a thesis statement, use it as the last sentence of their introduction, and then repeat it in their conclusions. In the majority of published essays—the sort of essays that students typically read in high school and college classrooms—authors tend not to simply conclude what they've already introduced. As noted in chapter 1, contemporary essays do not follow a five-paragraph structure. Instead, those writers take stock of what they've been able to claim and the evidence they have evaluated for those claims and draw logical, clear, and effective conclusions based on that evidence.

The grading rubric published by the College Board for the SAT offers similar criteria for a superior essay:

- Effectively and insightfully develops a point of view on the issue and demonstrates outstanding critical thinking

- Is well organized and clearly focused, demonstrating clear coherence and smooth progression of ideas
- Exhibits skillful use of language, using a varied, accurate, and apt vocabulary
- Demonstrates meaningful variety in sentence structure.

One of the key qualities of a superior essay, then, is the demonstration of both "insight" and "outstanding critical thinking." Again and again in our classrooms, we see those essays that are bound to a rigid, one-or-the-other thesis failing on exactly that point of the rubric. Instead of thinking through an issue or exploring it thoroughly, students who only mechanically reproduce a memorized formula spend their time simply generating evidence for something they've already (and often arbitrarily) made up their mind about. This rarely leads to insight, nor does it allow the student to demonstrate any kind of true critical thinking.

In contrast, students who allow themselves to think about the issue from a variety of perspectives, who are willing to ask themselves, "How is this more complicated than it might appear?" consistently show both insight and the ability to think critically about a wide variety of topics. Of course, an essay that possesses "outstanding critical thinking" but an incoherent structure or inappropriate or irrelevant reasons and evidence will not be judged "superior," but, at the same time, a bland, robotic response reflective of little care and less thought will likewise not score well.

We want students to engage in real-world writing and embrace the complexities of an argumentative prompt. As shown, this can be done through rich dialogic curriculum. Still, we want to level the playing field and make sure our students are prepared for standardized tests. Although we would argue spending too much time on this work is not worthwhile, it behooves us to consider exploring the required rubrics and example writing with students. For instance, Dawn and Dirk both invite students to break down the rubric of a standardized test. Students figure out what the rubric means and how it describes writing in order for students to understand what is expected of them. In this way, students analyze the rhetorical context of the writing situation, identifying their audience and purpose for their work.

Moreover, many standardized tests offer sample writing and scores for review. We know that students can grow in their own writing when analyzing writing. Why not have students also analyze sample standardized test writing and score the writing for practice? They can then compare their scores with the actual score and reasoning behind this score. In this way, students can practice evaluating writing to in turn apply this skill to their own writing. If students can evaluate other writing, then they can surely turn their attention to evaluating their own as well and get a better sense of self-monitoring and self-evaluation as needed for not only a standardized writing context, but other writing experiences as well.

AUTHENTIC READING, AUTHENTIC WRITING

The more we read, the more likely we are to discover that good writing follows no one particular formula. An excellent essay may be as carefully considered as E. B. White's "Once More to the Lake" (1941), as personal and metaphysical as Annie Dillard's "Transfiguration" (1985), as apparently discursive as David Foster Wallace's "A Supposedly Fun Thing I'll Never Do Again" (1996), or as seemingly paradoxical as Andrew Sullivan's "What's So Bad About Hate" (1999). What those examples share is a commitment to complication and a willingness to explore rather than ignore.

Last year, a student in Dirk's class reading George Orwell's "Shooting an Elephant" (1950) was incredulous that Orwell could state his thesis in the seventh paragraph of his essay. This, he said, violated everything he had been taught about persuasive writing and about "the essay" form itself. Why was it okay, he asked, for Orwell to save his thesis for the middle of his essay? Why, for that matter, he pointed out, was it okay for Annie Dillard to merely imply her thesis at the very conclusion of "Transfiguration"? Why, as he ultimately asked, was he required to state it explicitly and only at the end of his first paragraph?

Why, indeed?

You're not required to do so, Dirk told him. It's an academic convention prevalent to a greater or lesser degree in different disciplines. While it is true that many writers state their thesis directly and fairly immediately, many others withhold their thesis until late in the paper. What's important, we discussed, is figuring out—as writers do—what will work best within a particular piece.

Dirk's class discussed Toby Fulwiler's (1997) assertions of the advantages of each model (thesis-first or delayed-thesis) and Dirk invited each student, in every paper, to decide individually to place his/her thesis where it would have the most impact, not simply where someone else told him/her to put it. After all, if the most important element of a composition is its relative adherence to a preexisting, static structure, it's probably not going to be a particularly thoughtful, mature, or insightful piece of writing.

Again, some early attempts at breaking free of this formula were messy. It can be difficult, at first, to imagine creating a structure that fits its content rather than trying to force content into the Procrustean bed of a preexisting outline. But, as students got more comfortable challenging their initial assumptions about the topics presented and questions raised in "persuasive writing" prompts, and as they allowed themselves to be more engaged with the potentially interesting issues contained in those prompts, they wanted to showcase their ideas in the best way possible. If their ideas no longer fit the formulaic model that had offered great comfort before (but little potential for growth), they found themselves willing to seek out better, more individual structures.

Instead of settling for a "one-size-fits-all" approach, they began to tailor their organization around what they wanted to say and how they might best say it. The more they practiced developing a new structure for each new piece of writing, the better they became at it.

They didn't need to leave behind everything, either. Essays do have a beginning, middle, and an end, and, just like a five-paragraph essay, the middle analyzes and comments on a range of evidence. The students' newer, more complicated essays did the same, but with more honest consideration of the prompt, the evidence, and their stance.

In time-limited situations (as on an SAT, for example), some students found it preferable to adapt their ideas to a five-paragraph outline, falling back on something they knew well. Even those students, though, now expressed frustration with doing so. In their words, they "wanted to do something different" and knew that they "could have written a more interesting essay" but didn't feel capable of doing so in such a short amount of time.

What this means, wonderfully, is that when given time to brainstorm, discuss, write, and revise, the students are more likely to take advantage of it. The students now have a new, and better, task ahead of them: Writing an authentically sophisticated essay in an on-demand environment. This requires students and teachers to stretch beyond a formula. This requires growth.

Still, veering from a formulaic structure can be scary. Dawn learned this firsthand when she was teaching a speech class to write *This I Believe* essays as inspired by the radio program (http://thisibelieve.org/). The elective class was not focused on preparation for a standardized test; rather, students were working on honing essay writing and speech delivery skills. This work, however, fell during a standardized testing window. Dawn remembers a proud junior bouncing into class explaining how he responded to the ACT writing prompt with a *This I Believe* essay. While Dawn feared the possible implications of this approach, the student felt fully confident that he had passed. And, indeed, he did. This experience reminds us that authentic, inspired writing wins.

And isn't this our goal? We don't need to practice a formula over and over—we need to grow. Rarely, if ever, does the real world call for an impromptu essay due in 40 minutes. Sure, there are occasions in college, the workplace, and our personal lives that require a quick written response, but those circumstances never ask us to stake a claim between "this" or "that" without an analysis and evaluation of all the options in between. Real writing asks us to consider deeply, to weigh various pieces of evidence, and usually to arrive at a nuanced stance that acknowledges gray areas between the binary ends of any spectrum. Our classrooms, and, yes, even our tests, can help prepare students for that.

IN SHORT

- Repeatedly practicing a formula helps students succeed at being formulaic but does not necessarily lead to better student writing.
- Many standardized writing prompts seem to demand simplistic, binary responses, but this does not have to be the case.
- Standardized rubrics do not, in fact, typically demand formulaic responses.
- Engaging in authentic writing, from start to finish, typically results in more complex, more personally meaningful and more persuasive compositions.
- Truly persuasive writing does not ignore complication and complexity.

Chapter 3

Civic Engagement and Responsible Argument in Digital Environments

The aroma of coffee surrounded me as I searched for a former student, now almost a college graduate. She had invited me for a visit to talk about "life." I'm always delighted and honored when former students think of me; I started to wonder how I got so lucky, or, rather, what about my teaching led this now adult to want to reconnect with me.

Iqra had been a student in my 11th grade American Literature class. When we chatted, she shared her plans to be a pharmacist and explained that science was her true academic interest. Still, she asserted that American Literature had been her favorite course in high school—and the most important one. I asked her why. She cited her interest in learning about various author's lives and blushed as she tried to remember the plot of The Great Gatsby, *but, eventually, she said it, the gem that continues to inspire my teaching practice: Our class study of literature and composition was relevant to her life. I was ready to leap out of my seat and exclaim to the world how I had arrived at teacher success, but I restrained myself.*

Together, we recalled that when our class engaged in a social awareness and action project called "This I Wish to Change," Iqra began her topic selection with an ideal worthy of a Miss America competition: "I will solve world hunger." I remember pressing her, instead, about what she truly cared about and could do something about.

Earlier that year she had been disappointed when she was not admitted into the AP Literature class because she had not fully understood our school's requirements in her early years of high school. So I asked her about that. She said she wished she had known and planned ahead her freshman year. After this prompting, she switched her topic for the project. Ultimately, she embraced that issue for her research and created a video to help younger students learn the AP course requirements in case they were interested in taking those classes in the future. Our guidance department played it the following year for our students as a reminder to help them know their goals and plan ahead.

As we discussed the project, I realized that new students entered my classroom already familiar with many of the publications my students had produced from this project over the years: from the team that created a self-help website designed for students at our school to manage stress levels to the student who wrote to Congress raising concerns over sex trafficking in the United States to the students who created informational posters about the impact of Zebra mussels on local ecosystems. I also realized most of my summer visits were from students who were affected by this work.

I learned a lot from Iqra that day. She reminded me of the importance of relating content to student lives and to challenge students to explore what they really care about. Iqra didn't mention our reading of literary classics, and when she talked about her one writing class in college, she described being glad she knew how to write papers. But she really lit up as she talked about life, her goals, and embracing the world around her. I beamed at her success.
—Dawn

Civic involvement usually stems from a form of communication, often that of the essay. Whether the purpose of an essay is to find out what we think, to persuade or inform others, to offer alternatives, or to provide a means of awareness, the essay serves as an agent for change.

Essays highlight important conversations of the time. For example, Ta-Nehisi Coates' (2015) essay mentioned in the Introduction, "Take Down the Confederate Flag—Now," rang across social media sites as the political climate sparked debate on the topic. In fact, most popular debates inspire an essay of some sort that becomes part of the conversation. The summer of 2015 was flooded with opinion pieces about Harper Lee's *Go Set a Watchman* (2015) on topics ranging from the authenticity of the text to the status of Atticus Finch as hero or antihero. This conversation is not new (Gladwell 2009), but with the publication of Lee's second book, it took center stage.

These conversations are rich in analysis of the novel's circumstances as well as the content of the novel itself. This is authentic writing with authentic purposes and audiences. And these new conversations contrast with the mundane five-paragraph essays many students write about *To Kill a Mockingbird* (1960), which have no real audience or purpose beyond the classroom.

The essay as a way to communicate information and advocate for change is not a new notion, of course. We might still view America as a British colony if not for Patrick Henry's "Speech to the Virginia Convention" (1775). Yes, it is a speech, but we read it to this day as an essay. Henry wasn't alone, of course. Thomas Paine's "Common Sense" (1776) also pushed the country toward revolution. Alongside Hector St. John de Crevecoeur's writings (1782) that gave colonists a sense of American identity, these writers motivated the people to fight for independence.

It was difficult to publish and influence public opinion then; however, with the advent of the Internet and social media, our world is now ripe for civic discourse and engagement. By opening the conversation to anyone with Internet access, the conversation comes with both strongly constructed arguments *and* plenty of falsehoods, such as Internet hoaxes or just plain incorrect information. The benefits outweigh the downside, though—especially in the classroom. Why?

The essay prompts response, and with the help of socially mediated spaces, conversations continue. The essay's role in civic discourse is important, but the role of *commenting* on essays may be even more significant. Comments on a news story, blog article, Facebook, or Twitter are now a major form of discourse in our culture. Some comments present sound, strong arguments. Some are fatally flawed.

> The essay's role in civic discourse is important, but the role of *commenting* on essays may be even more significant.

Teachers can play a vital role in guiding students toward active, responsible, and intelligent civic engagement with essays and related online writing.

ARGUMENT IS EVERYWHERE

Learning is purposeful, authentic, and rich when we tie it to what matters most: Our lives. As learners, we build connections by relating content to our lives. We can help students expand their interests and discover relevancy in new places, such as through contemporary essay reading, as chapter 1 notes, and by asking them to observe the world around them.

As it turns out, noticing the world around you does not come naturally. We all know people-watchers and artists who imagine the stories of others, but most people need to be taught how to observe through different lenses. In Dawn's expository writing class, one assignment invites young writers to observe the world around them. The first time she gave this assignment, a student explained, "I can't do this assignment; I'm traveling to another state this weekend." The assignment was not typical of "school," and the student had to be reminded that observation can happen away from home.

How do we teach students to observe? One way is to take students on observation walks. Borsheim and Petrone (2006) describe their process of inviting students to "make 'meaningful observations' of their school" (p. 78). Borsheim and Petrone encourage students to explore issues from their world—their school—as a way to read "their school and community as 'texts,' pushing them to bring to light and call into question aspects of these 'texts' that normally remain invisible and go unquestioned and unchallenged" (pp. 78–79).

Many of the authors of this book use this practice with students, including taking students on an observation walk. If students look, for example, at athletic commemorative bricks, they immediately raise relevant questions: *Who purchases these? How do they decide what to put on the brick? What values are established with the bricks and the messages on them?* At Dawn's school, bricks often honor former students or teachers, but one brick reads "Here lies Dobby, a Free Elf." When students notice that brick, they identify potential arguments:

* Our community values literature and pop culture and playfulness.
* Anyone can write what they want on these bricks if they make a big enough donation.
* That brick was here to make our school famous; after all, a picture of it appeared on reddit.com.

An observation walk can lead to dozens of such topics. Students may note that the school community sends a message when only certain values are displayed on posters or when trash isn't picked up after lunch. Taking an observation walk with students supports multiple learning targets including exploring argument, questioning why and how a message is conveyed, and observing how everyday interactions also convey a message.

As they read the world around them, students begin to develop observation and critical thinking skills. Students have many texts thrown at them on a daily basis. If they do not stop to analyze and reflect on an advertisement (a topic chapter 4 discusses), for instance, it's possible they might be unwittingly convinced of a message. Moreover, if students start to see the world around them, it might spark some thinking and, perhaps, a desire to change it.

INQUIRY: ENGAGEMENT AND ARGUMENT

Students need to engage in conversation with one another and to write and reflect, share ideas, dialogue, and refine ideas yet again.

Teachers can embrace questioning and exploration through activities like observation walks and purposeful questioning, as well as through thoughtful dialogue, as chapter 2 discusses. Students need to engage in conversation with one another and to write and reflect, share ideas, dialogue, and refine ideas yet again.

Though not new, the notion of connecting student learning to student lives has a renewed focus. In 2013 the Connected Learning Research Network (CLRN) explored the way that teens learn in both in- and out-of-school settings, through exploration of interests, friendships, and social media. Scholars from the CLRN and Digital Media & Learning Research Hub (Ito et al. 2013) defined *connected learning* as an important move for student engagement and authentic learning. Connected learning is

> a model of learning that holds out the possibility of reimagining the experience of education in the information age. It draws on the power of today's technology to fuse young people's interests, friendships, and academic achievement through experiences laced with hands-on production, shared purpose, and open networks.

When teachers allow students to conduct inquiry into their own interests—and to do so by using technology to produce hands-on projects—students are now active in a participatory classroom that engages them and invites them to do something instead of just playing school (e.g., Garcia 2014; Jenkins and Kelley 2013; see also digitalis.nwp.org).

It's no surprise that when students in our classrooms are offered a learning opportunity that integrates connected learning principles, they embrace it. In Dawn's classroom, students explore essential questions focused on culture, engage—with support—in questioning and inquiry, and purposefully use digital tools. This work is highlighted in *Research Writing Rewired: Lessons that Ground Students' Digital Learning* (Reed and Hicks 2015). With this approach, students ultimately use their own curiosities and rich learning about their interests to compose an inquiry-based research essay and repurposed media response. The written essay maintains its status in the classroom but is situated with real purposes and audiences for the writing, as well as additional media work, to engage students in meaningful learning.

Dawn facilitates student inquiry with prompts for discussion; with the use of various mentor texts as models for arguments, essay, and media compositions; and by providing further information related to the topic of study. A teacher may use various methods in the classroom. Using dialogue and questioning techniques appeals to students' interests and allows them to set the conversation focus and construct authentic inquiry. Also, there are several platforms that allow teachers to support inquiry and student questioning by incorporating technology, such as blogs, wikis, discussion forums, and more.

Youth Voices is one specific community writing space that works well to support student writing, publishing, dialoguing, and collaborative thinking around inquiry. The Youth Voices community (youthvoices.net) is a site for conversations guided by teachers and based on the pedagogical approaches of participating teachers. The space is a place where "we invite youth of all ages to voice their thoughts about their passions, to explain things they understand well, to wonder about things they have just begun to understand, and to share discussion posts with other young people using as many different genres and media as they can imagine!"(Youthvoices.net).

One way inquiries happen through the Youth Voices community is through self and world questions, as inspired by Beane (1997). Teachers in the Youth Voices community invite their students to develop self and world questions based on their interests. (For a guide see: http://youthvoices.net/questions.) This work is often a springboard for more conversation.

Through the Youth Voices website, discussions can happen across schools—instead of just inside one classroom—and lead to better questions that students want to explore. Similar to units constructed around essential questions (Smagorinsky 2007) or the use of questions in teaching, as inspired by scholars like Socrates, Wiggins, and McTighe (2005), and Burke (2010), inquiry affords students the opportunity to dig into questions from their lives and to explore topics relevant to their world.

For instance, Patrick Henry's "Speech to the Virginia Convention" (1776) has its place in studying American revolutionary literature, but a discussion on Youth Voices may help students see that Henry's words apply across time and contexts too. His speech could serve as a springboard for considering the recent Egyptian revolution, including analysis of related news stories and social media activity. A Youth Voices discussion of Henry's speech could also lead students to examine the role of the written word in a democracy, and help them make connections not only to full-blown revolutions like Egypt's, but also to smaller, daily changes enacted by the written word. Students may refer again to the aforementioned Ta-Nehisi Coates (2015) essay about the Confederate flag, or to debates about gun control, police brutality, or health care. Ultimately, Youth Voices provides a community writing space that allows students to further develop their own stances by discussing online with each other.

Through implementation of connected learning principles and engagement in inquiry, teachers can integrate analyzing, questioning, thinking, researching, and reading throughout the curriculum. The essay is no longer a one-hit wonder but a means to communicate in thoughtful and engaging ways. This is indeed the type of discourse we want students to engage in, and it is a way to support skills necessary for essay writing. No longer does writing an essay need to be one solitary writing experience; rather, through reflection, writing in digital spaces, journaling, and more, students can engage in more complex, extended analysis.

> The essay is no longer a one-hit wonder, but a means to communicate in thoughtful and engaging ways.

ARGUMENT IN DIGITAL ENVIRONMENTS: CONNECTED COMMUNITIES

With digital writing as the way of writing in our world today, civic engagement opportunities are easily accessible. New platforms mean new modalities of writing, such as the 140-character tweet. They also mean new opportunities for writing, like the collaborative writing spaces offered by wikis or Google documents. These new options offer opportunity for students to explore argument and engage civically by entering various relevant conversations. Moreover, all learners now have spaces to connect with others for personal learning networks on various interests, from gaming to recipes. We can support student learning about appropriate discourse in these online spaces by practicing the analysis of conversations within these spaces and having them enter the conversations of today. A few platform options are noted in Table 3.1.

ACTIVISM AND ENTERING THE CONVERSATION

The essay is only effective when it reaches an audience; therefore, we need to consider civic discourse and the role of activism in our classrooms. This is writing that *does* something that takes action. Wilhelm, Douglas, and Fry describe this type of work in K-University settings in *The Activist Learner: Inquiry, Literacy, and Service to Make Learning Matter* (2014). Wilhelm et al.'s position that we need to construct curriculum with inquiry and service learning at the heart provides a means to embrace connected learning. As they note, "The results of these relationships create lasting, personal connections that make transformation possible" (p. 102). They also argue for the "shared responsibility" we all have in this world.

Work from various scholars supports this notion of service as important not only to our democratic society but also to literacy learning (Bomer and Bomer 2001; National Writing Project 2006; Winter and Robbins 2005). For real change to happen, students have to determine appropriate rhetorical situations for their compositions, whether working in print or in other media formats. With activism and service learning, students may also be producing various texts in both print and media formats.

Principles of connected learning are supported with work in digital environments, as they support student engagement in civic conversation happening in online spaces, from news sources to blogs, to social media. As we've all seen, some of these conversations are rich, but some are laden with poor arguments and falsehoods. We need to teach students to enter the conversation in purposeful and powerful ways, through knowledge. We want our

Table 3.1 Platforms for Digital Communication

Digital Tool Platform for Communication	Audience and Purpose for Writers
Blogs: An online journal. Modality requires writing in shorter sections, including hyperlinks to outside sources, and incorporation of visuals.	Published online, the audience can be anyone (though private settings are possible in some blogging platforms so that posts can be restricted to only one specific group of people). Many blogs focus on attracting specific followers with a similar interest in the topic of the blog. The purpose is to share ideas and spread information. This is also a publishing opportunity and chance to evoke change, share opinions, or challenge ideas.
Wikis: Open-source spaces where many people can add content. As with all digital writing, layout and format are key, headers and use of images and hyperlinks are an important part of this composition.	Wikis, like blogs, can be open to anyone or restricted to a specific group of people with membership to the wiki. The purpose is to collaboratively create materials, though often one leader may develop the content for the website, as wikis are also used at times as a website platform. Through this site, writers can work collaboratively to create content. Wikis also often have discussion features to build dialogue with either wiki members or anyone reading the wiki website.
Google Apps for Education: Google documents, as well as slides and forms, offer opportunities for collaborative writing or review of print documents, visuals, presentations, or even the creation of surveys such as through the use of forms.	Google Apps are only available when shared with others, but there are ways to also publish work from Google through embedding into other websites. Collaboration purposes are essential for use within this platform. Writers and readers can collaborate through composing together or leaving comments for one another.
Twitter: 140 characters to compose in a social networking space. Tweets may include a message to share content with followers or a retweet (sending out another writer's message again). Hashtags or #topic offer the opportunity to categorize content to enter conversations with the bigger Twittersphere.	Twitter is designed to share information publicly so anyone can follow you, favorite, or retweet your ideas. The purpose is to disseminate information. Ultimately, sharing ideas or evoking change through the sharing of ideas is a part of this platform.

students to be the writers prompting reflection on an essay or refuting a point, as careful critical readers and smart savvy writers. As Kenneth Burke suggested (1973), entering the conversation includes first understanding the conversation. In his metaphor he notes that eventually, participants will join the conversation and "decide that [they] have caught the tenor of the argument [and] put in [their] oar" (pp. 110–11). In this way, we too want our students to have the background and wherewithal to enter the important conversations of today and "put in their oar."

Teachers can guide students as they enter these conversations. From social awareness and action projects such as the "This I Wish to Change" assignment, to mentor texts such as "Humans of New York," or supported educational curriculum such as TED-Ed classrooms, to educational partners such as with news media source KQED and the KQED Do Now program, teachers can engage students in compositions for civic engagement that employ connected learning, inquiry, and activism. Each of these projects will be described below.

This I Wish to Change

"This I Wish to Change," as described in the opening vignette, is an assignment focused on research, inquiry, social awareness, and action. This project could be incorporated into almost any unit of study, but Dawn uses it with her American Literature class's study of *The Adventures of Huckleberry Finn* (1884). While reading Twain's novel, students explore the purposes of his writing. The role of satire and realism are considered, as well as the prompted question of whether or not his book is about change or awareness. Students are then invited to explore what they care about in *their* world, from either a local, national, or global standpoint. After researching their topic, students explore whether or not there is something they can do to address the topic.

As students read and reflect on their topic, they designate their own audience and purpose for their work. They also determine their own modalities or products based on the audience and purpose. Students are challenged to not only explore what they truly care about and inform themselves but also figure out how to enter the societal conversation on the topic. Students write for professional purposes and write in a variety of genres.

One student, for example, wrote a letter concerning early school start times to the school board. The composition laid out a Toulmin Model argument in the genre of a letter. The following school year, the entire student body was surveyed about school start times as the school board considered the issue. Other projects include pamphlets made available in the school library or guidance office on various topics from domestic violence to discrimination to body image. Other students engage in media work. One student created a TED talk conversation about health and AIDs education. Another wrote a letter to the French government challenging a specific public response to racial discrimination toward a woman who was forced to remove her burqa in a public setting. Others write to Congress or create websites to promote awareness and conversation related to their topic.

In these authentic projects, students grapple with the various sides of a conversation and the gray spaces in between. Alina, the student who wrote to the French government, understood that the woman who was asked to remove her burqa was at an airport, and the concern was over public safety; yet she also understood that the action devalued her Muslim culture. This is not an easy issue to take a position on—if accurately informed. Nevertheless, Alina wrestled with the information and composed a strong argumentative, yet congenial, letter to the French government. She also joined digital conversations related to her topic, such as with her comment on the blog site https:// abidnyc.wordpress.com.

Alina raised awareness by sharing her research and letter with our school community. However, Alina's stance faced opposition in Dawn's class, as all students did not understand or respect the Muslim culture and beliefs (see figure 3.1). Alina demonstrated her conviction—and dedication and conviction toward justice—by working harder to educate her peers about Muslim culture while remaining professional.

Alina Aglia *says:*

May 12, 2011 at 5:44 am

I have recently just done a social awareness project on the burqa ban in France and it was brought to my concern also how immoral the burqa ban is. Women wear the burqa out of preference, and it is not a sign of enslavement as most believe. The quran does not state that is it mandatory to wear it, however, it does encourage the wearing of it. It is an independent choice, and the government should have no authority to ban it in my opinion.

Reply

Figure 3.1   Civic discourse inspired by Alina's research

This work not only promotes change for the audience, but it also changes the students who engage in the work. It changes thinking. Nina, a student who believed her future role was to become a doctor because they make a difference and make a lot of money, didn't actually care that much for science.

In a high-performing community, being a doctor is the norm in many conversations. However, when she started her project, she became curious about her experiences as an African American female in a high-achieving school compared to students in a neighboring, yet supposedly low-achieving school. So, she began her journey as a junior in high school exploring educational inequalities.

She explored issues of income inequality and testing bias. After writing an essay to solidify her beliefs, Nina turned this work into a presentation, contacted the local university and presented her information to a university class focused on equal education opportunities. The following year in an expository writing course, Nina continued her interest by exploring similar issues as well as educational systems in other countries. She wrote an extensive research paper on the topic, and then repurposed her work in collaboration with a team of other students interested in educational issues.

These students created a documentary highlighting various issues related to education and a call to action to improve the educational system in the United States. By the time Nina graduated from high school, she had an extensive reading list related to education inequality and she enrolled in college as a political science major anxious to tackle this issue.

Clearly, Nina offers an example of a student thoroughly engaged in her work, but no matter the scale of the work, students can make small waves of change in their communities and themselves as they engage in activism and conversations relevant to their communities. By choosing their own interests and appropriate rhetorical situations for their work, students also engage in developing powerful compositions focused on awareness and change from their own experiences and exploration of local, national, and global issues. They learn a lot about their communities and issue of focus, which in turn supports their development of responding as a civically engaged citizen. Skills required of an essay and argument apply to the various forms of writing—narrative, professional letters, professional informational texts, arguments, film scripts, and so on—students engage in. This work is becoming even more possible through various digital platforms.

Humans of

Narrative story can create argument and lead into various forms of essay writing, including media arguments and the incorporation of visuals. "Humans of New York" (http://www.humansofnewyork.com/) began with one writer cataloguing people from his city with photographs and stories. This rich opportunity to capture life and the stories within it has inspired some of our colleagues in Red Cedar Writing Project to take up similar work with their students.

Aram Kabodian, middle school English teacher at MacDonald Middle School in East Lansing, Michigan, and Elizabeth Cyr, high school English and journalism teacher at Stockbridge High School in Stockbridge, Michigan, began their own respective "Humans of Greater Lansing" and "Humans of Stockbridge" programs. Following the blog model of Humans of New York, their students interview people from their community and compose an image and description of that person's life. Aram's students work is highlighted in Humans of Greater Lansing online at http://humansofgreaterlansing.tumblr. com/and Elizabeth's students share their writing at http://uncagednews.com/category/humans-of-stockbridge/.

While this informational writing is one of story, through story arguments also emerge, such as with one student who discovered after interviewing several females from her high school that they were plagued by low confidence. With that story, this student raised awareness of the concern and found a writing niche to continue to explore as an activist by starting her own column in the school newspaper. In these middle and high school classes, students are exploring "Humans Of" to both report on culture and shed light on humanity.

TED Talks

Technology, Entertainment and Design (TED) talks began with a focus on "ideas worth spreading." The conversations on TED have been so rich, they are often learning opportunities for all students. TED-Ed (http://ed.ted.com/) supports teachers in sharing lessons and supporting students in creating their own TED Clubs and TED talks. Creating TED talks is not an easy process, as the speaker needs to care about their topic, know about the topic, and plan a deliverable essay to support their ideas. Students in Dawn's class often select this modality as a way to transform and repurpose their research and share their insights on various topics from their inquiry work. Topics have included gender inequality, stress, acceptance of others, and the role of science fiction in projecting future development.

The student TED talk reprinted in Figure 3.2 highlights ninth grader Mingxuan's connection between a literature circle reading of *The Curious Incident of the Dog in the Night-Time* by Mark Haddon and bigger inquiry questions Mingxuan was interested in, specifically how people with autism understand their cultural surroundings.

TED-Ed, the Public Broadcasting Service (PBS), and National Public Radio (NPR) offer support for educational curriculum as well. NPR's *This I Believe* series (http://thisibelieve.org/) offers numerous fruitful essays that tell personal stories, often engaging in civic topics. StoryCorps (http://storycorps.org/) also offers wonderful models of sharing stories, like that of Humans of New York, but with an additional focus of capturing the story with an audio recording.

Picture living in a world like this: Where every movement you make is calculated, every activity that goes on around you is keenly observed, and every thought flitting through your mind is completely fact-oriented.

That's the world through the eyes of an autistic person.

Now picture living in a world like this: Where every new place you visit is a complicated and confusing maze of buildings and roads and stores, where you constantly struggle to understand what other people are trying to tell you while you struggle to convey your own ideas, and where sometimes, due to your overly keen senses, you're completely overwhelmed by an onslaught of sounds, sights, smells, and touches.

That's the world through the eyes of an autistic person in American culture.

"I find people confusing. This is for two main reasons. The first main reason is that people do a lot of talking without using any words. The second main reason is that people often talk using metaphors."

That's one of the first things Christopher, the main character of The Curious Incident of the Dog in the Nighttime, tells us. People on the autism spectrum take things very factually and literally, so they don't get jokes and idioms and metaphors. They don't take physical cues like we do either. The social tendencies and way of thinking of our culture isn't one that autistic people understand easily. The next time you have a conversation with someone—a face-to-face conversation, not one using technology—pay a little more attention to your body language. I bet you'll be surprised at how much you move your arms and hands, and how many things you convey through facial expressions. We do things like that naturally, without needing to think much about them. To people with autism, all of these things require a conscious effort to do and pick up on when other people do them.

Now, let's think about another aspect of culture. When I say big city, what's the first thing that pops into your mind? I, for one, think skyscrapers, hustle and bustle, lots of people, things like that. Big cities like New York and Chicago also symbolize the modernity and technological growth in American culture. Let's be honest here, we're a pretty loud country, both in terms of sounds and sights. Think about all the flashy signs and advertisements we see everywhere we go, and the bombardment of noise we experience every day, from traffic sounds to music on the radio. Even when we think it's silent, there's always that clock ticking in the background, or those annoying sniffles and coughs you hear from that one person. Now, think about what it would be like if all those sounds and sights were amplified five times, and you never could catch a break. That explains why some people with autism groan, cover their ears, throw tantrums, and do other strange behaviors, doesn't it? Their senses are on overload, and while we cope by just going to a quieter place, or squinting and covering our eyes, they can't. Because that's what they experience, every single moment.

Figure 3.2   Mingxuan's script for her TED Talk *(Continued)*

> *Now, I've put autism in a pretty confusing light here. Autistic people may have a different perspective than us, but that isn't necessarily a bad thing. They don't lie, they never cheat, and they don't judge people based on their outward appearance, as we often do. They observe all the details we never take the time to slow down and notice. They have their own sort of culture, and there are aspects we can learn from them. As I once read on a website called "Autism Speaks", don't view autism as a disability, but rather a different ability.*

Figure 3.2   Mingxuan's script for her TED Talk

KQED Do Now

News sources engage conversation. KQED, a Northern California public media station, developed a pilot program in 2011 called Do Now, which was described as "a weekly activity for students to engage and respond to current issues using social media tools like Twitter" and "aims to build civic engagement and digital literacy for young folks" (KQED). The program grew with support from the National Writing Project, Educator Innovator, Twitter, and several other media and education organizations. Today, KQED produces Do Now activities twice a week on current events in the news, arts, and sciences and reaches thousands of educators across the country.

KQED Do Now, an opportunity any teacher can offer to students, begins with a question for students to consider, followed by brief background information, audio or visual media addressing the topic, and links to additional information. Students respond to the weekly topic on the blog or in Twitter posts with specific hashtags, as well as other social networking platforms. Additionally, students are invited to also create media responses to the question and to share a link to their original work. Through this work, students enter conversations related to relevant news topics with an authentic conversational purpose and an authentic audience of anyone online and, even more specifically, students across the nation engaging in this same work.

Students working with KQED Do Now's weekly civics, science, arts, and pop culture conversations engage with media and literacy as they use technologies for professional learning, so work with KQED Do Now offers an opportunity for students to build civic literacies with multimedia tools. These conversations support connected learning principles, offering authentic and engaging learning opportunities.

While civic discourse has its own merit, participation in KQED Do Now can support several other curricular objectives as well. Carrie and Mitch, for example, have both used KQED Do Now in essay writing classes. The Do Now posts and responses themselves are generally brief, but the rhetorical skills students take from the activity are highly transferrable; students learn to support a position with sound reasoning and to better anticipate counterarguments as they engage in real discourse about real issues with real people.

KQED and Literary Connections

Dawn has found that current events also relate to various texts of study in her classroom, supporting an integrated approach to using nonfiction in the classroom. For instance, when her class was studying *To Kill a Mockingbird,* a KQED Do Now civics question was "How can we prevent Veterans from being homeless?" This prompted discussion related to poverty in the novel and the treatment of people living in poverty. When her class read *Romeo and Juliet,* a KQED Do Now civics question was "Are Schools Teaching Sex Ed Too Late?" During the exploration of this question, students related the content to the education needed to support healthy relationships, education that perhaps Romeo and Juliet would have benefited from.

In 2014 during the Winter Olympics in Sochi, Russia, students in Dawn's American Literature course were studying revolutionary literature. The Olympic Games have had a political connection since they began and this year was no different. As such, KQED Do Now centered a weekly civics discussion around politics and the Olympics. As part of this Do Now conversation, students were invited to compose a digital media project that could be shared as part of the KQED Do Now conversation focusing on the Olympics. This was a natural complement to the study of revolutionary literature that allowed students to make cross-text connections while reading the world around them.

Exactly how did this work? Students read about the Olympics and discussed the coverage, studying print media, film, and images. Students were then invited to select one text about the Olympics to read closely and offer a rhetorical analysis of the piece. Additionally, students knew that the audience was global and that the rhetorical analysis would be shared with the KQED Do Now audience. After students selected their text for analysis, they read it carefully for the role of message, audience, purpose, and author's craft. Students also selected a technology for the purpose of analyzing this work and going public by sharing their work with the KQED Do Now audience.

Students explored various options for how to share their thinking through screen shots of their annotations of digital texts and video notation software. Once students closely analyzed their text and decided how to share their work with a specific technology, Dawn's class developed a collaborative wiki that highlighted each student's work on a separate page. The entire class work can be found at http://olympicstextanalysis.wikispaces.com/. Some students crafted their rhetorical analysis right on the page, simply linking to their text and writing their response on the wiki page. Others embedded images, animated gifs, video, and marked up digital print texts. The KQED Do Now conversation for this topic can be found at: http://blogs.kqed.org/education/2014/02/14/olympics-political-dissent/.

KQED Do Now and Synthesis

In this way, students create media arguments in response to the civic conversations. Additional media responses could be interactive timelines, infographics, films or remixed media, and the Do Now topics cover a wide range as well. Dawn's students used Mozilla X-Ray Goggles to respond to the question of whether celebrity obsession is bad for us, remixing images to highlight ways that our culture is obsessed with celebrity. For instance, two students, Shiazore and Zach, collaboratively changed a headline about Princess Kate Middleton's wardrobe from "Kate Middleton Wears Red Striped Coat in Scotland: Get the Shoe, Clutch Details" to "Celebrities Wear Expensive Clothes Everyday: Shocking" to highlight that all celebrities wear expensive clothes.

Other examples of this work can be found at http://blogs.kqed.org/education/2014/05/20/is-celebrity-obsession-bad-for-us/. Media responses to a topical conversation offer opportunity to explore argument creation in various formats and consider the ways in which visuals and media also create and support arguments. The work of commenting and media responses is the analytical discourse we want and need students to engage in as thoughtful readers and writers in our world today.

KQED's media-making resources for students and teachers support this work in the classroom, and with the KQED Do Now Roundup—a compilation of the weekly conversation assembled by the KQED Do Now staff—teachers and students can synthesize the material. When Dawn's student's created a KQED Do Now Roundup, they approached the work as a genre study. Then they explored media they would include on the page, and through collaborative learning the students embraced research skills, relevant analysis, and synthesis of content, all the while being engaged and motivated to do the work. Additionally, as students dug into the conversations, they were becoming even more civically informed with their work. Frequently, students turned to Dawn to note that they were excited to explore other areas of interest. Dawn's student's Do Now Round Up can be found at http://blogs.kqed.org/education/2014/11/20/requiring-voters-to-show-id-can-be-a-complex-issue.

Engagement with current issues supports students' development as democratic citizens. With these types of relevant learning experiences, students develop analytical skills and hit learning targets noted in the CCSS. It is key that teachers provide opportunities for students to join worldly conversation.

INVITING STUDENTS INTO THE CONVERSATION

In 2014, the Black Lives Matter movement became a major topic of civic discourse. Teachers have a responsibility to engage students in civic discourse and offer spaces for them to converse meaningfully about such events. If we're reading novels or nonfiction about race issues in the past, how can we ignore the news of today? The weekly Teachers Teaching Teachers conversation on the Ed Tech Talk channel (http://edtechtalk.com/ttt) offered a forum for teachers to converse about this topic, and by fall of 2014 students from various states—New York, Utah, California, and Michigan—were joining the conversation. Dawn's students readily embraced the conversation to learn different perspectives. Students who originally were not interested in positioning themselves quickly discovered the complexities of such topics.

Teachers have a responsibility to engage students in civic discourse and offer spaces for them to converse meaningfully about such events. If we're reading novels or nonfiction about race issues in the past, how can we ignore the news of today?

Inspired by such conversations, students engage in conversation on Youth Voices Live (http://youth-voices.net/live) as they explore various big questions. Through dialogue students enter into the truly complex issues relevant to their lives. How do they get there? They are invited into the conversation and supported in their development of questions and use of evidence to support their ideas. By inviting students into conversations and structuring conversations for students to explore topical issues, students can find their way into the conversation, they can put in their oar and engage in civic discourse and action.

IN SHORT

- Relate content to student lives. Expand student connections through careful questioning with students.
- Recognize argument in the world around you. Find it and question it with students.
- Embrace inquiry, curiosity, and the research process to explore interests and build knowledge.
- Explore activism opportunities driven by students.
- Take advantage of digital tools that offer opportunities for authentic writing experiences.
- Analyze mentor texts and join conversations with news sources.
- Invite students into the conversation. Support students in their reading, writing, reflecting, and talking about key issues in the world today.

Chapter 4

Exploring Argument from Multimodal Sources

During the early years of my career when I was teaching 8th grade, I attempted to spruce up a conventional poetry lesson by creating an entire music-themed unit. I knew I was not the first teacher to use music as a real world gateway to appreciating poetry, but, as a musician on the side, I figured this was a great way to connect with the students both as their teacher and regarding the content.

To get the ball rolling, I engaged my students in a debate that would eventually lead to an argument paper on whether file sharing was a positive or negative in the music industry. At the time, Napster was the name most associated with free file sharing and was stirring up controversy as to whether or not it should be legal. To kick start the debate, I used an opinion article from my trusty middle school subscription to Writing! *magazine leftover from my predecessor.*

Reader, Karen Lerman (2001), wrote about the benefits of services like Napster. In it, she makes comparisons between file sharing and loaning CDs to friends and concludes her piece by demanding that any musicians who have a problem with file sharing "should think about why they started making music in the first place" (15). Besides some of the unsubstantiated facts of the piece regarding CD sales, I was truly troubled by the self-righteous nature of the tone. Who made her an expert on why musicians make music? My band, Palexia Went to England, certainly loved playing music, but we also knew that making albums was not cheap in the days before personal recording software. There were studio costs, manufacturing costs, and annual fees for selling online.

More alarming was how convincing this girl's argument was with my students. They blamed musicians for being greedy and assumed they were all millionaires simply because they had name recognition. Even more amazing were the misconceptions many of them had about the law. Inspired by the author's point about sharing CDs, many students claimed file sharing was fine because it was no different than burning CDs for friends. They were surprised when I told them that burning CDs for other people is illegal. There was a simple logic in play that if technology provided the means for something, then it must be legal. This girl spoke confidently so there must not be any flaws in her opinion, right?

Over a decade later, students have become more aware of the legality of the issue as the debate evolved. But what about new issues that surface today? How will today's students avoid the same problem? Arguments based on incorrect assumptions and overconfidence are nothing new, but this experience pointed out a need to change direction in how I teach argument writing.

Students need to do more than simply make a claim with reasons for feeling that way. There needs to be purpose and not just to get what you want. There needs to be an understanding that assumptions do not count as prior knowledge. Most importantly, arguments should not be based solely on what students know, they should be based on what students will know after they fairly assess what information is missing. The best way to do that is to explore the multimodal arguments that surround students every day, not just the arguments on a piece of paper handed out by a teacher.

—Dan

In some ways, education is overly simplified as a "monkey see, monkey do" process. Teachers demonstrate how something is done, and, in turn, ask the students to replicate it. Obviously, there is more to education than that. While there is no room for varied responses when adding two and two, that is not the case with writing instruction, which requires a great deal of modeling.

As described throughout this book, teachers use mentor texts, but also as explained throughout this book, there is no one correct way to write and therefore the number of mentor texts is limitless. Thousands upon thousands of writing samples exist that don't fit the five-paragraph mold. In fact, it seems like that formula was created as an afterthought. While this produces a variety of writing instruction from classroom to classroom, no teacher sets out to create masters of mindless replication. The goal is not only to have students create meaningful writing but also to understand and recognize when they do or do not see that same required purpose or completion of thought in other writing. This could not be truer or more important than with argument writing.

> Students are being equipped with an important set of skills not to enter the "real world" but to take the real world back to school.

Before Dan begins his first lesson on argument writing, he does not tell his students that it will prepare them for the "real world." In fact, he says the opposite. In the "real world," people fail to follow the expectations of successful arguments. People falsely imply, lie by omission, confuse confidence or heartfelt opinion with fact, and persuade by means other than the facts. And as the introduction pointed out, persuasion is not necessarily argumentation. What Dan does tell his students is that they are being equipped with an important set of skills not to enter the "real world" but to take the real world back to school.

THE PHANTOM ARGUMENT

When commercials for The American Society for the Prevention of Cruelty to Animals (https://www.aspca.org) appear on television, there is an emotional appeal from the very beginning, but are such advertisements factually supported or are they mere persuasion? Most of the commercials are comprised of photos with occasional text about the abuse of animals. The most stirring part of one of the organization's more notable commercials is the accompanying Sarah McLachlan (1997) song, "Angel." Unless your heart is made of stone, you instantly feel sorrow and empathy for the animals featured. According to an interview with the *Huffington Post*, even Sarah McLachlan herself has to "change the channel. It's just so depressing" (Brekke 2014).

Advertisements present an interesting angle to the world of argument. They are typically brief but have more "extracurricular" argument tools at their disposal. Are clips of animals in cages done in slow motion because it causes you to look longingly into their eyes or was it simply because the animals would not sit still long enough? Is the song manipulative? If so, does that make the cause dishonest? Not many would argue that the SPCA is not a noble cause or that its commercials do not include relevant information, but you can see that the emotional appeal of its claim is mostly due to elements that have nothing to do with anything resembling evidence. While it is collecting money for a worthy cause, this is a nonprofit organization. So what about commercials using similar tools for companies looking to make a profit from viewers?

When a shoe company spends 30 seconds telling you how light its new basketball shoe is while playing a montage of performance highlights from the professional athlete spokesperson, does it successfully present an argument that meets all of the requirements of an English assignment? Assume the claim is "You should buy this." It is then reasonable to follow that the main piece of evidence is the shoe's weight. But that's where the argument ends. It is where too many arguments end, not only in commercials but also in everything from editorials to the political arena.

As the works of Toulmin (1958), Hillocks (2011), and Smith, Wilhelm, and Fredricksen (2014) would emphasize, this commercial is missing a crucial warrant. A follow-up to the evidence. An answer to the question, "So what?" Or is it, in fact, missing such a warrant? Does the weight of this shoe mean that the consumer will be able to do everything shown in the montage? Is the montage full of slow-motion slam dunks to give the illusion of weightlessness or is it simply because real time moves too quickly?

The hope is that most people are not gullible enough to believe that a shoe will turn them into a professional athlete and that all of this is a moot point. But it still has not answered the question as to why weight matters. Do most people even know how much their old shoes weigh in order to make a comparison? If weight matters, are basketball players better off wearing no shoes at all? Obviously, there is no expectation for a commercial to respond to every possible counterargument or any possible counterargument for that matter. However, students in the classroom are consumers and should ask themselves, "Do advertisers provide the reasoning that, say, my teacher expects of me, or do I make it up in my head for them?"

Arguments are not always in writing. When they are, students can find what the author is claiming and hope that the reasons for the claim are also in writing. However, in the technological age, students can find that all of their senses are being bombarded such as in commercials. When this happens, they can't simply ask, "What is the author saying?" They may also need to ask a series of questions:

- "What is the author showing me?"
- "What is the author playing for me?"
- "*Why* is the author doing that?"

While there is nothing wrong with preparing or conditioning people for an argument (i.e., setting the mood or sales pitch), it is important that students separate that conditioning from the argument itself.

OPINION-FACT HYBRID

In Stephen Colbert's first episode of *The Colbert Report* (Drysdale et al. 2005), he introduced the world to a new word (or an old one with a new definition, actually) that embodied a recognizable era of fraudulent argument. "Truthiness" was cleaned up by the American Dialect Society (2006) and became Merriam-Webster's 2006 word of the year (2006).

Truthiness (n): the quality of preferring concepts or facts one wishes to be true, rather than concepts or facts known to be true.

While the Federal Trade Commission enforces laws regarding false claims in advertising, what protects us from truthiness or from what "just feels right?" What happens when claims are supported by popular opinion? Is it considered fact if almost everyone believes it? What if that popular opinion has been known to change over time like a fashion trend? Is it still considered "fact-ish" for now? Here, again, is where we begin to dance in that gray area. The complex world of thought that requires more of us but leaves us better off for it.

In a series of print ads created by Ogilvy and Mather (https://www.ogilvy.com) for Benzac AC, an antiacne cleansing cream, the viewer is required to interpret the entire argument being made because there are no words other than the name of the product. Clearly, the creator of the ads paid attention in class on the day metaphors were taught. Each of the three ads in the series features a solitary person physically separated from different, enjoyable social situations such as a pool party or a dance by what appears to be giant acne, as if the scene takes place on the surface of someone's skin. Unless Earth acne is a new consequence of global warming, it is safe to assume that this is the metaphor. Once again, we can assume that the ad is claiming a need to purchase the product. But why?

In one of the three ads, a solitary girl stands on one side of a gigantic zit. On the other side of Zit-zilla is a male character sitting alone in a convertible under a moonlit sky and gazing over the city landscape, an area more commonly known in a variety of B-grade movies as "Makeout Point." (This ad is easily found through a Google image search of key words "Ogilvy" and "Benzac.") The acne is literally preventing the girl from being with the boy. Metaphorically speaking, is that why this ad claims a need for this product? Does acne prevent girls from enjoying romantic evenings with a significant other? Regardless of the answer, there now exists a debate more exhilarating than the original claim.

When Dan presents this ad to his class, that piece of "evidence" inevitably comes up and usually very quickly. Just as quick is the handful of groans of disgust for its superficiality. When he asked his class if people should be judged by the clearness of their skin, the students unanimously gave a resounding "no." However, when those same students were asked if they agreed with the evidence as a fact that acne inhibits dating, twenty-eight out of thirty agreed. Because, there was even a small disagreement with the statement, the "evidence" should have immediately been placed in the "claim" pile as a different debate waiting to be proven for another time. Yet, here it is pictured clear as day.

In addition, if it is now classified as a claim or opinion, then how did such an overwhelming majority of the class come to agree with it while, at the same time, not wanting to agree with it? There was once a world before anti-acne cream and mankind managed to survive. So what changed? Where did this conflicting definition of beauty come from? Students were now grappling with questions that they didn't readily have the answers to. The lesson had quickly become one in which students were debating the complex overlapping worlds of reality and perceived reality. They were using the same tools as before but now the class was actively trying to find a solution to a question as opposed to proving a solution they already had in mind. They were truly arguing. At this point, what does a teacher do with the original assignment that started all of this beautiful chaos? Actually, nothing. The lesson has gone someplace different, someplace better.

When we recognize the complexity of arguments as more than just a choice between two sides and allow students the chance to explore further down the rabbit hole to more layers of debate, those discussions inevitably become student led because of growing invested interest. And their enthusiasm to engage with each other is more valuable than the original assignment. Dan's class may have been tasked with identifying the required elements of a proper argument in an advertisement, but it led to a more enthusiastic practice using those elements in a verbal debate on a related but different topic.

In today's world of education where teacher evaluations may require stating objectives at the beginning of a lesson, teachers may be wary about going "off script." But perhaps Holden Caulfield was on to something when, in *The Catcher in the Rye* (Salinger 1951), he describes his fondness for digression.

> What I mean is, lots of time you don't know what interests you most till you start talking about something that doesn't interest you most. I mean you can't help it sometimes. What I think is, you're supposed to leave somebody alone if he's at least being interesting and he's getting all excited about something. I like it when somebody gets excited about something. It's nice. (pp. 184–85)

This is true for today's students as well. While there is a need for purpose in the classroom, there is always room to veer off in another direction when the class stumbles upon something more purposeful. To deny enthusiastic learning for the sake of staying on task may not only be an unfortunate loss of opportunity, it may be downright difficult to do. Sometimes solving one problem means having to solve another first. As Holden says, "I mean he'd keep telling you to unify and simplify all the time. Some things you just can't do that to. I mean you can't hardly ever simplify and unify something just because somebody wants you to" (p. 185).

Teachers need to be aware of the urge to simplify. In the race to fit two tons of curricula into a school-year-sized box, it is possible that teachers skip complexity in favor of quick answers. In the episode entitled "Much Apu About Nothing" (Cohen 1996) on the popular series *The Simpsons*, the convenience store clerk, Apu, studies to become an American citizen. During his oral exam, he is asked for the cause of the Civil War, but as he begins a complicated answer of "numerous causes" including abolitionism and economic factors, the examiner interrupts Apu and urges him simply to say "slavery." While it has a comedic effect on the show, educators need to make sure that the time crunch we all feel during a school year doesn't lead us to become "the examiner" in our classroom.

In other words, school is a place for students to enlighten their thinking. When students are confronted with an argument, are we encouraging them to work through the problem, allowing them to build on their knowledge and understanding of the world, or do we force them to simplify once they demonstrate an ability to complete the assignment? Are we grooming them to think for themselves or to simply develop a talent for identifying and saying what people want to hear, leaving them to rely on their gut?

THE PREFERENCE ARGUMENT

While successful arguments do not allow a stubborn clinging to the "right to my opinion" in the face of glaring facts and evidence contradicting that "opinion," it is possible for successful arguments to involve all parties holding true to their original claims after all evidence is put out there (Rouner 2015). What determines these arguments' success is the same factor that determines the success of an argument where everyone walks away in agreement: Understanding.

It is not possible to prove that someone's favorite food is not as tasty as yours but it is possible to understand why his preference is different. There could be scientific evidence suggesting his genetic disposition to enjoy salty or sweet tastes is different from yours. It could simply be because it is a sentimental and comforting reminder of his childhood. In most cases, preferences cannot be proven incorrect. Instead, the goal of arguments like these is to come to a better understanding of every position taken or simply to explain yourself. As long as preferences do not cause harm in any way (in which case they could be considered incorrect), coming to an understanding of them is a valuable ability in a world filled with a variety of cultures and customs.

Our own pop culture supplies us with plenty of opportunities for preference arguments. When Francis Ford Coppola re-released the movie *The Outsiders: The Complete Novel* (Frederickson 2005), he changed almost the entire soundtrack, a movie score that was composed by his own father. Instead of instrumental pieces, the movie played to the sounds of Elvis and

Jerry Lee Lewis. Why did he change it? It could not have been an easy choice considering the family connections to the original. Clearly, he thought the new soundtrack sounded better. But does it? And what do you do with those opinions?

An even more challenging and debatable set of examples deals with alterations to a movie itself. When Steven Spielberg issued the twentieth anniversary edition of *E.T. the Extra-Terrestrial* (Spielberg) in 2002, he made changes to both the dialogue and what the viewer saw. He altered a line where the mother tells her son that he cannot go out for Halloween as a terrorist and he digitally altered guns used in one of the final scenes into walkie-talkies. Was this a sensitive promotion of nonviolence in a post 9/11 world or an over-reactive ruining of a movie that millions love?

And what about the Star Wars series? While there have been more changes and digital alterations than the average person can keep track of, fans often point out the famous shootout between Han Solo and Greedo the bounty hunter. Many people interpret the original as Han shooting Greedo in cold blood in order to get away. The newer alteration clearly shows that Greedo shoots first making Han's firing look like an act of self-defense. While it didn't affect the outcome of the shootout or the plot in any way, many fans felt it changed the character. Are they right? In a 2012 interview with *The Hollywood Reporter*, George Lucas said he always meant for Greedo to fire first and that now he simply widened the shot to show it (Block 2012). Does that make it better? Should perceptions of the movie be forced to change even if they were incorrect to begin with?

How much control should a creator have over his creations after they have been embraced by popular culture? There is no denying that people grow attached to characters. These attachments are not limited to the big screen. Should the language in *The Adventures of Huckleberry Finn* have been cleaned up in a later release, or should we face the ugly past of a nation? Should J. K. Rowling have revealed as nothing more than a side note ten years after the release of the first book in the Harry Potter series that Dumbledore is gay (Siegel 2007), or does a more LGBTQ friendly world make it irrelevant? Can readers ignore the existence of Harper Lee's *Go Set a Watchman* (2015) in order to preserve Atticus Finch as the icon of justice and equality they had come to love in *To Kill a Mockingbird,* or are they required to redefine the character?

Despite being fictional worlds, lovers of reading have learned that these worlds are capable of exciting us or letting us down within a short period of time or even decades later—much like reality. Students have to grapple with this dilemma in real life. While teachers can present literature as art worth appreciating, the discussions and arguments that literature creates even outside of the book itself is great practice for coping with real-life surprises and disappointments.

In Stephen King's *The Dark Tower* series, King inserts a brief author's note before the final pages of the final book, *The Dark Tower* (2004). In it, he warns readers to reconsider finishing the book if they are content with the situation of the main characters up to that point (pp. 817–18). Because it took decades for King to finish the series, no fan of it would ever consider stopping that close to the end. However, King presented a sudden final theme, a last-minute argument ripe for discussion. Should we be careful of what we wish for? Is ignorance bliss? Is knowing sometimes worse than the suspense of not knowing?

The biggest frustrations in life usually come from a lack of understanding. For that reason, the goal of an argument isn't to win but to understand and be understood. So how do we teach the art of understanding? Is it a vague concept that we can only hope students comprehend? No, but it takes some practice. Today's world seems to condition students to always take a side, to believe that there is always a correct answer, and, as chapter 2 discusses, to write confidently like they picked the right one.

> The goal of an argument isn't to win but to understand and be understood.

Maybe they confused the message when they were told one too many times in middle school to stop ending papers with "That's what I believe. What's your opinion?" It certainly seems like students are always required to defend a position in traditional writing prompts or responses to a standard article. Multimodal arguments like the examples mentioned earlier are a means to break the mold. The trick to writing with the purpose of being understood is for the writer to be clear that this is how he feels only and to avoid challenging the reader's interpretation or feelings on the subject. In other words, avoid making claims that the reader must fall in line with.

But how can you have an argument without a claim? The argument is one the student has with himself. "Why are my preferences or interpretations what they are?" Just as with abstract concepts like love, a writer cannot always put his finger on why he feels the way he does about things. The claim in this argument is the writer's attempt to figure it out. It has nothing to do with anyone other than himself. This means there are no statements which speak for people in general such as "The song creates a feeling of . . ." Instead, "The song causes me to feel . . ." It is a very personal style of writing that may seem foreign to the argument genre.

However, movies, music, and art require interpretation and that interpretation relies heavily on personal context. For one person, a song may be beautiful due to its association with a classic Hollywood movie scene or with a first date. For another, it might be grating to the ears due to its being overplayed in a fast-food commercial or its association with an ex-girlfriend. More so, these different interpretations might apply to the same person through different periods of his life.

When Dan has his students work on understanding, he directs them to find one of their favorite songs and write a preference argument about why they like it. The only instructions are to avoid speaking for everyone and to focus on why the writer likes the song, not to defend it as a good song. The instructions are simple, but the writing is usually easier said than done. Students rarely have any difficulty expressing their opinions or preferences. Not all preferences, however, appear logical to wider audiences.

When a student claims that the songs of a specific heavy metal or "screamo" band are his favorites because he finds them relaxing, he is now battling an audience whose mainstream definition of "relaxing" does not match the loud, intense, sound of this style of music. The student is now required to explain (i.e., provide a warrant) for this seemingly glaring contradiction which may not be easy to do or even be understood by the student himself. Efforts to be understood in arguments such as this one cannot use "just because" as a sufficient warrant any more than in an argument made in a debate on foreign policy or gun control or religious exemptions.

In one paper, a student sets the stage for a very similar need for an explanation:

> If I am in a sad mood, normally I will listen to a country song, and this is a very wide range of songs, and I don't particularly have a favorite. But it's kinda an oxymoron because most country songs are sad so they tend to make me even sadder. I do always like a song by a list of singers, George Strait, Alan Jackson, Brad Paisley, Blake Shelton. It does somewhat calm me down when I am sad.

While "oxymoron" may not have been the word he was looking for, it is clear that the student recognizes that his audience may not understand his choice of music for sad moods when he points out how "they tend to make me even sadder." Why does he want to lean even further toward that end of the emotional spectrum? While he does hint at a positive calming effect, the student needs to further explain how sadness helps him through sadness. Or does he?

It is important to point out that this student made a claim perhaps without even realizing it. By describing sad country songs as an odd choice for a sad mood, he is basically stating that sad people normally want to be cheered up. Is that always true or is this a completely new preference argument topic? At this point, the teacher could instruct the student to revise the paper to remove this assumption. But why risk throwing out a much more engaging path of introspection that the student has already begun traveling down just for the sake of saving the assignment topic? Instead the next draft of this paper should focus on a new topic: Cheering up versus Embracing Sadness.

In another example, a student explains why "Home" by Phillip Phillips is her favorite song:

> This song reminds me of my journey moving from Michigan to North Carolina, and eventually moving back to a small town in Michigan. When we moved in 2012, it was just my brother, mom, and I. It seemed like we dropped everything and moved away. After a few years, due to a death in the family, we moved back to Michigan but to a different town than before. Because so many changes happened in such a small amount of time, I became deeply connected to my mother more than I ever had before. This song was one we played almost on repeat throughout the adventure because it was a reminder that we are home, not solely based on location, but whether or not us three were together.

This is a perfect example of the uniqueness of preference arguments. A person may absolutely hate the song but find it hard to argue with this student's personal and touching final line as a reason for her appreciating it as a great song.

By focusing on understanding, students can more easily see that arguments are more complicated than mere "yea or nay" debates. An emphasis on understanding also highlights a primary stumbling block to good thinking and writing because it helps students see that claims are dependent on one's experiences and point of view.

THE GOLDILOCKS ARGUMENT

Students should never learn that the simple solution to an argument is to "agree to disagree." This does not mean that they should argue claims until they are blue in the face. After all, it will be necessary from time to time to walk away from an argument if stubbornness from one side prevents the debate from being productive. Or, as in the case of a preference argument, the goal is to be understood more than it is to agree. But not every argument is a preference argument. Sometimes a decision needs to be made. A conclusion needs to be met. Information needs to be shared. Participants in an argument should not be let off the hook and allowed to voluntarily dismiss factual information. This is a predicament very clearly explained in Jef Rouner's blunt and appropriately named article, "No, It's Not Your Opinion. You're Just Wrong" (2015).

However, it is possible for both sides of an argument to present numerous pieces of convincing evidence. When that happens, it is important for both sides to come to terms with all of the evidence. Look at some of the major debates of the last century. Topics like the death penalty wrangle with concepts that individually outside of the debates are most likely important to everyone: human life, justice, civilized society, economics, deterring crime.

However, when you can't have all of them in the context of the argument, prioritizing them becomes the debate.

But they do not become less important. In fact, it would be disingenuous to pretend that they no longer matter simply because they hinder your case. It is important for students to acknowledge opposing evidence and reckon with it. The difference between right and wrong is not always clear. We know the Nazis should not have built concentration camps. We know that Rosa Parks should not have been arrested for sitting in the front of a bus. But what happens when we ignore the complex gray area of less obvious debates?

In Jon Ronson's book, *So You've Been Publicly Shamed* (2015), Ronson addresses the problem that is created when people use social media to voice their opinions as absolutes. The reach and anonymity that social media provides creates a safe space to ignore context, counterarguments, or even factually correct information. It can be a place for people to ignore the human element and seek a Hammurabi "eye for an eye" type of justice. When that happens, people can often receive a punishment that outweighs the proposed crime. Because social media is such a huge part of our students' lives, it is important that they learn how to approach arguments in a social media context. Unlike in the classroom, a Facebook post or tweet most likely will not provide a point/counterpoint allowing our students to make a well-informed decision.

News organizations are often to blame for these poorly constructed arguments because they provide a headline and ask social media viewers for their opinion based on that alone. Students need to understand that the information needed to take a well-informed position in an argument is rarely handed over on a silver platter. They need to develop skills for asking questions and seeking information that fills in gaps in order to make a fair assessment rather than, as this chapter addressed, trusting their guts and setting out to win despite what they stumble across along the way. They need to gain prior knowledge through modern essays and media.

One viral video (Voluntaryist 2013) that made its way around social media involved a 21-year-old driving through a Tennessee DUI checkpoint on Independence Day. With a camera in the passenger seat recording the exchange, a situation escalated when a highway patrol deputy greeted the driver and asked him to roll his window down farther to which the driver responded by saying, "This is fine, sir." The driver went on to ask if the surprised officer's follow-up questions were required. The officer grew frustrated and eventually the driver was asked to pull over and a search was done on the car. Through occasional text narration, the video claims that the driver was within his rights to act in the manner that he did and that the consequences were unconstitutional. Implying greater concern, the video ends sarcastically with the text, "Happy 4th of July, America."

An argument is being made with this video that civil liberties are violated in America. Assuming that all of the legal text throughout the video is accurate for the sake of this argument, it seems clear that the officer was in violation of procedure. One West Virginia news organization, WOWK 13 News, which shared the video on Facebook, clearly considered it shocking content by adding the comment, "WOW, look at this!" (July 8, 2013), but is that the end of the argument?

Can a case be made for the officer? Even if he is wrong, is it possible to understand his actions? How often does someone refuse to roll down his window at a checkpoint and why would he do so? The officer is clearly caught off guard by the driver's response. Regardless of whether or not the driver was required to obey the officer's requests or answer his questions, were they unreasonable? Does it matter that in a video released later from the officer's dashcam, the driver is heard saying he understands the officer's reason for suspicion?

So, is it possible for the officer to be wrong and right at the same time? It is if we embrace the complexity of the argument. But why should students do that? In this case, it affects what viewers of the video take away from it. The officer may be in the wrong as the video states, but understanding the officer's actions may debunk the grandiose nature of the claim that America is entering a police state. With understanding, the officer is no longer an absolute villain and civil liberties are no longer in danger. In the end, neither side of the argument was proven entirely right or wrong. Instead, both sides of the argument came to a mutual and more accurate assessment of the situation. This can be called a Goldilocks-style middle ground. While understanding may not have affected a need for the officer to receive consequences, it may affect what those consequences are.

There is an important disclaimer when adding "understanding" to an argument. Understanding can easily transform into mistaking opinion for fact if certain parameters are not added. Much like with the rules for a jury, understanding should not be based on speculation. It should be rooted only in the evidence available. One could easily speculate that the officer acted out of frustration from having to deal with a difficult driver after a long night of looking for drunk drivers instead of being home with his family on a major holiday.

While you might easily find this to be a possibility, it is because you suspect that you would feel that way in his shoes. While it is possible that it might be true, there is no evidence in the video to suggest he hates working on holidays or that he even has a family to go home to. Therefore, we cannot assume it when judging the situation. However, we do have video of his reactions and audio of what he and the driver said, including the officer's explanation for pulling over the driver. We also know that most of the half hour of detainment was spent talking calmly. In other words, why would a video seek an emotional response from its viewers that was never present (with the exception of the initial officer response) between the two parties actually involved in the incident?

When the evidence of this multimodal argument is dissected, we are left with more than just the two choices of law-breaking police officer or trouble-making kid. It could be possible that both choices are true just as much as it is possible that neither is true. If the goal of this argument is to find a solution that helps to avoid incidents like these, then it is important to properly identify all of the problems. Put another way, if a car isn't roadworthy, you don't just blame the engine when the tires are flat, too.

SO WHAT NOW?

When students are given a prompt or an article to respond to, they assume they have all of the information needed to complete the assignment. They apply prior knowledge and trust that the information provided by the teacher is sufficient. In most cases, they are correct. Teachers want their students to develop an ability to process information. The author of a piece of writing can get creative with wordplay and tone to appeal to a reader, but creators of multimodal arguments like those mentioned earlier in this chapter have many more tools at their disposal that our students need to be aware of. Camera angles, soundtracks, images, editing. They complicate arguments and make them more appealing at the same time.

Arguments are not as simple as categorizing everything as right or wrong, good or bad, and important or unimportant. Cameras can view events from 360 different angles. Why should our students be limiting themselves to viewing things from two? Our students not only need to be able to process what they see and hear, they also need to consider what they do not.

> Cameras can view events from 360 different angles. Why should our students be limiting themselves to viewing things from two?

These multimodal arguments surround students every day. Their ability to create these multimodal arguments increases as improvements in technology make the tools accessible to the common man, which makes it all the more important for students to understand arguments and how multimodal texts influence us. They say that the pen is mightier than the sword. Nowadays, so are video cameras, television, and the Internet. And just like pens and swords, they can be ineffective or even costly if you don't know how to wield them knowledgeably.

IN SHORT

- Arguments are influenced by more than just words on a sheet of paper. Do a check on all five senses.
- Students' reactions to claims are based on what they were told, what they already know, and how they feel, which could be incomplete, limited or inaccurate, and emotionally biased. Teach students to know what they don't know.
- Don't be too quick to judge digression because some arguments require layers of critical thinking. As Hemingway once said, "It is the journey that matters, in the end." Do you really need a solution that badly to the argument topic you assigned?
- When using a preference as an argument, the author needs to decide what he hopes to achieve from the argument. Is it to prove he is witty and aggressive by creatively "burning" the opposition? Or is it to be understood and move the argument toward a potentially needed compromise? The "you struck last, now it's my turn" psychology of human beings doesn't really allow both to occur and so preference arguments need to be written accordingly.

Chapter 5

Creative Writing as Argument

"Oh! I remember that book!"

"I love Dr. Seuss!"

"Yes! Are we reading that, Ms. Nobis?"

I smiled at the enthusiasm of my high school seniors and knew I had made a good choice. After weeks of reading essays and excerpts from other nonfiction texts, my students were losing steam. Because I didn't want to lose them, I knew it was time to mix things up a bit. With the AP English Language and Composition exam looming just a few months away, I had to keep them focused and engaged.

"Yes," I told them, waving a copy of Dr. Seuss's The Lorax *in my outstretched arms. "It's story time!"*

The students, accustomed to rearranging the classroom to fit the day's activities, quickly moved their desks into a semicircle reminiscent of the "circle time" set up in my own child's kindergarten classroom and prepared to listen.

I love picture books, but I had never thought to use them in the high school classroom until I had children of my own. My husband and I, both AP Lang teachers, couldn't help but probe our then-four-year-old with questions as we read to him: Why do you think the illustrator used only black and white on this page? Why is there only one word on this whole page? What makes this page seem scary? *Our son's answers ranged from insightful to "I don't care," but the experience led me to consider the responses my seventeen-year-olds might give.*

Anything can be rhetorically analyzed, and students can mimic the good techniques in their own work. Creative texts—even picture books—are no exception. In fact, much can be gained by reading and thinking critically about a wide variety of texts. I had listened to colleagues explain to me that

AP Lang was a "nonfiction" course so often that it hadn't occurred to me yet to supplement the course anthology with anything other than nonfiction.

But it worked. Perhaps because the students weren't intimidated by the text, or perhaps because the brightly colored illustrations awakened something in them, but for whatever reason, my students jumped into the richest analytical discussion we had had all term, and their subsequent written rhetorical analyses were equally rich. Dr. Seuss had helped my students see that all writing can—and often should—be critically analyzed. Best of all, there were smiles around the room all hour.

At the end of the lesson, one of my students joked, "I'll never be able to look at a picture book the same way again, Ms. Nobis!"

And I knew I had done my job.

—Carrie

In addition to showing students that essays can (and should) use personal voice, innovative structure, and narrative examples, teachers should also show students that readers are persuaded by far more than essays. We already read fiction, drama, and poetry in English classrooms. We can encourage our students to see how well-written creative works make as much of an argument as an essay, and we can help students see how they might use the rhetorical tools of fiction writers, poets, and playwrights to make their own arguments. Embracing creative writing is clearly worthwhile in its own right (Robinson 2011), but it also helps students break out of formulaic patterns to write better essays.

Take argumentation, for example. It is most obvious when it comes with the clearly defined structure of claim, evidence, and reasoning. Obvious is not the same as effective, though. There is a reason English classes have emphasized fiction and poetry through the years: We humans live through story. We identify with characters and see ourselves in stories. We don't often identify with or see ourselves in essays, though, so arguments may be most effective when they are not even essays at all. Fiction and poetry can change a reader's thinking as much or more than essays can (Mar and Oatley 2012).

This book has asserted throughout that the notion of an "essay" as something with a strict structure or a set number of paragraphs or even one particular style is outdated or misguided. When we stick to this outlook, we miss the chance to welcome students to the conversational form of the essay itself. Since Montaigne, one use of the essay has been to reflect, to ruminate on one's thoughts publicly.

Anyone who asks students to write their own *This I Believe* essays has already jumped into narrative essays. Anyone who requires students to write reflections at the end of the term is engaging students in metacognitive self-analysis. But all too often, teachers get bogged down in covering the "basics" of essays, and students graduate having written only staid literary analysis and stilted arguments. There is room in a student's K-12 education—and certainly in one's college years, as well—to explore the creative sides of essay writing.

COMMON CORE AND CREATIVITY

If an essay is an attempt to come to an understanding of a particular topic or to express that understanding in an interesting fashion, then there is no one right structure, no one right style, and no one right voice for said expression. Many teachers of high school juniors and seniors find themselves teaching some form of the "college essay" or offering students feedback as they attempt to write their application essays.

In Dirk's high school, located in a suburb of Washington, DC, English teacher William McCabe has his seniors draft and revise what he calls a PLASS—a Positive Life-Affirming Short Story. In these pieces, students must convey an understanding they have of the world, or of themselves, in a concise, engaging way. These are certainly essays, even if few of them have explicit thesis statements or force their content to fit a set number of paragraphs.

As they prepare to graduate, Dirk's senior English students complete a lengthy essay exploring themselves in relation to the works they have read and the experiences they have had over the course of their last year of high school. There is no one right way to complete the assignment, nor is there one particular style that's better than another. Instead, each student must find a structure, a voice, a style, and an approach that works best for him or her— one that best fits both the student and his or her content.

Sharon wrote her final paper as a three-part meditation on her life in high school, incorporating several genres, allusions to and passages from six different works she read in class. The different vignettes in the paper discussed her relationship to her education, to her friends and family, and to herself and demonstrated, throughout, not only a clear understanding of the significant ideas of her chosen novels and plays, but also a deep and learned appreciation for how the different writers reflected in her piece manipulated literary elements and rhetorical tools for effect. In a segment entitled "Drowning" (Figure 5.1), Sharon alludes to both *Waiting for Godot* and *A Visit from the Goon Squad,* writing of the seeming paradox of her need for organization and structure and the potential emotional paralysis that can result from such intense scheduling.

Many teachers worry about spending curricular time on creative writing. They shouldn't. Dirk's student may not write this sort of prose poem in a formal academic essay, but she certainly can employ the techniques she used

> Everything is boxed into its own concrete existence, allotted its own portion of time, balanced out to the ounce. Perfect. Some things get more attention than others, and at times, some get none at all. Don't need this? Toss it away to conserve time and space in the brain. Day in and day out, I go through these processes—in my head, on paper, in motion. It's a constant whir of organization and the completion of tasks.
> **But habit is a great deadener.**
> Sometimes it's quiet; sometimes I do everything and still lack closure.
> Then I wonder:
> Why I don't feel anything. How there is no excitement or fulfillment to be had. How "not sad," the numb midway between happiness and sorrow, can really suffice as an emotion. How I can lose the desire to be around my friends and family. How I can truly have nothing to say to someone anymore. How I can explain the emptiness growing inside me, eating up what once was cheerful and full of passion.
> I think back to my flurry of organization—of boxing, folding, stacking everything so it sits in its own pre-allotted place. No room for deviation or flaws.
> Somewhere along the way, I threw what is important into the pile of "to be sorted" and it got lost. I filled my life with tasks and facts and duties and nothing more.
> I took my passion and **folded it in half. Then in half again, so I hardly felt it. I could slip it inside my pocket and forget about it, with a feeling of safety and accomplishment.**
> I got rid of what truly makes me me.
> At least I checked things off my to-do list. At least there's that.

Figure 5.1   Excerpt from a student's final senior English paper

both to analyze the works of Samuel Beckett and Jennifer Egan and to decide how best to communicate her understanding of those works to an outside audience. Besides, time spent developing students' creative voices need not "take time away from the curriculum" as many concerned teachers say. In fact, the CCSS can offer support to help teachers not only keep fiction and poetry in the classroom but also potentially increase the amount students are reading of each. As our students read more creative work, and as their teachers invite them to try the same rhetorical techniques in their own writing, their writing will improve.

THE CREATIVE SIDE OF THE COMMON CORE

But how can the CCSS help? The standards brought a renewed interest in using nonfiction in English classes because they suggest a 70/30 split for student reading across the school day: 70 percent nonfiction and 30 percent fiction. This has led to an increase of nonfiction in English classes. It should be noted that this is at least in part a misreading of the CCSS (Gallagher 2015) because the 70 percent nonfiction represents *all* reading in a school day, not just in English class. Unfortunately, many schools have interpreted this to mean they must replace fiction titles with nonfiction. Goodbye "To Build a Fire," and hello "The Declaration of Independence" in English class.

But that's wrong. Good nonfiction benefits students, but English courses should not jettison fiction. Raymond Mar and Keith Oatley (2012) have shown that the simulative experience involved in reading fiction expands a reader's own empathy and experience base. The brain assimilates rich narrative similarly to actual lived experience. A Stanford study (2012) showed that reading literary fiction increases overall cognitive functioning as well. That's a lot of bang for the reading buck.

Teachers need not ditch fiction, and, in fact, many teachers should add fiction and poetry where it's currently lagging. At Mitch's school, for example, students take five classes per term in a trimester schedule with only two terms of required English classes. On average, that means over the course of one school year, only 13 percent of most students' classes are English courses. If anything, schools need to *add* fiction and poetry to both English *and* other courses.

How can English teachers keep literature when a misreading of the CCSS has led others to cut some of it in favor of nonfiction? By drawing clear connections between good literature and writing lessons that can improve students' argumentation. Creative writing can connect good literary reading with good argumentative writing.

> Teachers need not ditch fiction, and, in fact, many teachers should add fiction and poetry where it's currently lagging.

For example, poetry can help students see how any text can be an argument. Ultimately, all writing aims to change the reader's mind, no matter what form the writing takes. Mary Oliver's poem "Morning" (1992) is an account of lessons Oliver learns while observing her cat. This may not aim to convince the readers to change their minds on a critical social issue like an essay might, but her poem does ask the audience to reconsider its approach to daily life. It alters the way the reader thinks about the importance of observation itself, about what we value as humans, about whether or not other species have life figured out better than we do, or even about the form of free verse poetry itself. Just as not every essay is written in five paragraphs, not every argument is written as an essay.

Also, students might be more engaged with argument, rhetoric, and the issues raised by the typical questions on standardized tests if they are allowed and encouraged to explore other avenues and genres of writing. When simply and repetitively plugging a thesis and evidence into a straightforward five-paragraph essay, students may not be developing into the writers and thinkers they need to become. We can change that. In our classrooms or even on standardized tests, we can encourage students to make their arguments in alternative ways. Teachers can help students explore writing from different angles, including narrative nonfiction, poetry, drama, fiction, comics, picture books, and literary analysis.

TEACHING ARGUMENT WITH PICTURE BOOKS

The CCSS require students to consider a text's "use of evidence and rhetoric" while "assessing the stance" of the writer. As noted, English teachers are often drawn to nonfiction to address these standards, but they need not be. Much of the reading our students engage in, both in and outside of school, is fiction; and picture books are some of the first texts to influence one's thinking.

Young children almost invariably love books, and this love is most often born on the lap of a loved one holding a picture book. Children love being read to, and they are eager to learn to read themselves. Teenagers can recapture that love in their high school English classes when their teacher shares a picture book with them.

Most of our students read Dr. Seuss when they were younger. The simple rhyme schemes, invented words, and imagined creatures can strike a sense of nostalgia, so when the teacher pulls *The Lorax* (1971) out of the closet, the atmosphere in the classroom immediately lightens, freeing students up for less inhibited discussion. In fact, the very term "analysis" can be daunting to high school students, and using a familiar text that is fun and less intimidating than those found in the course anthology allows students to focus on the elements of rhetoric and argument.

Often when students hear the word "argument" in the classroom, they conjure up images of five-paragraph essays and ACT prompts. As English teachers, we know that this narrow view of argument is incorrect and potentially dangerous. Our students need to understand that they are exposed to—and influenced by—argument all the time.

The following activity demonstrates to students that creative texts like picture books can present very compelling arguments. While one could analyze the purpose and rhetoric of any picture book, Dr. Seuss's ubiquity and almost universal appeal make him a good choice. Plus, Seuss has several books with clear sociopolitical stances, including *The Lorax*, *The Sneetches*, *Yertle the Turtle*, *Horton Hears a Who*, and *The Butter Battle Book*, that could complement a variety of thematic units. Sharing one of these books makes it easy for students to see that creative genres can be powerful venues for argument.

THE LORAX AS RHETORICIAN

Carrie chose to include *The Lorax* in a unit focused on environmental issues. To begin, the teacher reads *The Lorax* aloud without showing students the illustrations. Students listen and take notes on what they *hear*. Separating the text from the illustrations helps students listen carefully now and will help them recognize the impact of the visual rhetoric later. It doesn't matter whether or not students are already familiar with the book; as with any text, the reader will respond according to his or her experience with the text at that moment.

After this initial reading, the students respond to and provide *textual* evidence for questions that help them focus their thinking on the author's purpose:

* How does Seuss want his audience to feel about the Truffula trees?
* How does Seuss want his audience to feel about Thneeds?
* How does Seuss want his audience to feel about the Onceler?

On its own, the text conveys a clear purpose, and students will pick up on that. Encouraging students to identify specific evidence to explain their response helps them understand the writer's craft and will eventually help them to more deliberately consider decisions in their own writing.

The second time the teacher reads *The Lorax*, she presents the illustrations as well. Students view the illustrations and take notes on what they *see*. Students then return to the questions posed earlier and offer *visual* evidence for their responses:

* How does Seuss want his audience to feel about the Truffula trees?
* How does Seuss want his audience to feel about Thneeds?
* How does Seuss want his audience to feel about the Onceler?

In the case of *The Lorax*, the images and words work together to create a stronger impression on the reader. After discussing this, students are ready to draw conclusions about the author's purpose and how the author goes about achieving his purpose. The following are questions to consider:

* What is the primary purpose of the book? Provide both visual and textual evidence.
* What is the overall tone of the book? Provide both visual and textual evidence.
* How do the illustrations enhance the book's rhetorical impact? Provide specific visual evidence.

- How does Seuss's diction enhance the book's rhetorical impact? Provide specific textual evidence.
- How, if at all, does Seuss appeal to ethos? Logos? Pathos?
- What other rhetorical strategies does Seuss employ in his text and/or illustrations?

After tackling some of the basic rhetoric of a picture book, students might surprise themselves by digging into deeper analysis. Because they are comfortable with the text itself, they are often able to see layers that they might not notice in other texts that require more sophisticated decoding. For example, *The Lorax* clearly advocates for protecting the environment, but many students will also see it criticizing corporate greed and consumerism. *The Butter Battle Book* takes on deeper significance when one considers that it was written in 1984, during the Cold War. When the text itself is not intimidating, students feel more confident exploring the context, syntax, images, and diction of a book. Students might research the emotions associated with different phonemes in an effort to explain Seuss's invented words or read up on the psychology of different colors.

The Lorax makes a compelling argument, causing even the youngest of audiences to think about something they might otherwise not have considered. Despite the absence of data, expert testimony, or clear rebuttals of counterarguments, the creative children's story has an impact on its audience. Perhaps the reader is not moved to act or to shift his or her point of view, but that, as this book has mentioned before, is not always the point of a piece of writing—even an argument. Simply getting the audience to consider a topic serves an important purpose.

Analysis of a picture book has its own merit. After all, our students read them as children, and many of our students will one day read them to their own children. Understanding the impact of these books is relevant to our students' lives.

However, bringing picture books into the classroom serves other purposes as well. For one, it demonstrates the general principle that creative texts make arguments, a principle that can be reinforced in students' own writing. This fact will not only help our students to consider novels and poetry and movies more critically, but it will also encourage them to designate and work toward a purpose in their own creative endeavors.

Finally, once students have found success recognizing the author's stance and the use of rhetorical strategies in a picture book, they gain confidence and are able to transfer these skills to other texts as well. In addition to learning rhetorical elements of an argument, fiction helps students understand the personal element involved.

ARGUMENTS IN ANECDOTES

Sometimes the best lessons can develop out of bizarre requirements. Often, poets say they write in closed forms like the sonnet because tight structural requirements challenge them to be even more creative. (Note: A tight structural requirement is not the same as a formula, and a sonnet is not a five-paragraph essay.) While this is certainly not always true of teachers crafting curriculum, there are times and places where standards and other requirements can help us combine lessons in creative ways. We can kill two or more birds with one stone, so to speak.

One example of this is the Advanced Placement (AP) English Language and Composition course that puts its focus on nonfiction and the essay, but many teachers, including this book's authors, have found themselves using fiction in AP English Language for a range of reasons. When Mitch was stuck with only a couple of weeks left in the term to prepare his AP English Language students for the transition to AP English Literature and Composition in the fall while also reinforcing argumentation skills introduced earlier in the year, he called on short stories. Fiction would allow him to do both at once. Reading like writers would help the students see how fiction's ability to create empathy relates to argumentation.

Mar and Oatley (2012) proved that literary fiction increases empathy in the readers. Literary fiction (as opposed to less immersive "light" reading) draws its readers in deeply and allows them to get inside characters' heads. Fiction also affects the readers' brains in such a way that our brains act as if they have gained the stories' experiences themselves. If you were to read a book about mountain climbing, your brain would then have some of the same experiential benefits of a person who had actually climbed a mountain.

This is a neat trick for something like mountain climbing, but when applied to emotional issues or social concerns, students can see the persuasive power of storytelling. Through reading fiction, students gain new perspectives. They don't just get wrapped up in plotlines; they get to know the characters, and, as a result, gain some of the characters' outlooks and experiences—to the extent that many students go on to write fan fiction stories to post online.

STORIES AS EVIDENCE

Too often, schools ask students to respond to a cold writing prompt without preparation. Using fiction to improve arguments prevents this problem because readers get to see the impact on a person. Good writing puts a name and a face to the issue, and techniques normally found in fiction writing can help students do that in their own essays by bringing narrative and description to otherwise potentially dull prose.

For example, Mitch often teaches Sandra Cisneros' commonly anthologized short story "Eleven" (1991) (a story that also showed up on the 1995 AP English Literature exam). It tells the brief story of Rachel being embarrassed by her teacher in front of the class on Rachel's eleventh birthday. A sweater has been left behind, and the teacher insists the smelly thing is Rachel's even though it isn't. It raises the importance of considering life from another person's point of view before acting. Rachel's teacher does not do this, and she brings Rachel to tears as a result.

After reading, students are usually furious with the teacher and sympathetic with Rachel. Why? Because fiction leads to empathy. Readers identify with Rachel feeling picked on. They remember being eleven and how even the smallest problems seemed monumental. Readers see the teacher as a bully because she doesn't listen to Rachel.

It is a short and seemingly simple story, but it can be mined for a number of arguments:

- How should a teacher interact with her students?
- How might students speak up on their own behalf?
- How could the average classroom better serve introverted students?
- What consequences might be applied when a teacher is emotionally abusive to a student?

These can lead to bigger questions too. Many of the problems in the story arise because of the arrangement and rules of a traditional classroom. Cisneros' four-page story about an eleven-year-old could easily lead to a deep argument about the benefits and failings of a traditional K-12 classroom.

Cisneros' story is told from an engaging first-person point of view. It is the story of an eleven-year-old's bad day, but it can also be analyzed with the Toulmin Model of Argumentation. Here is one way that might look:

- Claim: Teachers should be respectful of students' feelings to ensure better learning.
- Evidence: Rachel cried in class and felt very uncomfortable in her learning environment. She said the sweater was not hers, but the teacher didn't listen. In fact, the teacher told Rachel to "put that sweater on right now and no more nonsense" (p. 8).
- Reasoning: The teacher ignored Rachel, which led to Rachel crying in class and not paying attention to that day's lessons. Had the teacher been more respectful of Rachel, she would be more emotionally healthy and would have learned more in class that day.

There are other ways to analyze the story. Surely Rachel could have been more vocal in standing up for herself. Her classmates could have been more supportive. Everyone involved could have just ignored the sweater in the first place. Regardless, analyzing the story as an argument will help students see that arguments are everywhere, even in stories, and that stories can also help readers think critically and build better arguments themselves.

Some teachers and standardized tests would merely demand students to write to a prompt like "What, if anything, should be done to improve the American school system?" When students come to such a prompt cold, they're likely to fall back on such larger, more general suggestions as, "Fund schools equally," and "Help students achieve their dreams." Reading a short story first, however, gives students many more ideas to run with, and often more specific ones at that.

The readers can't help but remember their own K-12 classroom experiences after reading about Rachel's bad day. Students could write about the story, as school often asks them to do, but literary analysis is far from the only option here. Using fiction as a lead-in to writing essays encourages the students to consider many of their own experiences that could support a claim. The teacher could assign a number of argumentative written responses next:

> Using fiction as a lead-in to writing essays encourages the students to consider many of their own experiences that could support a claim.

- Short story: Write your own fictional story that elicits an emotional response from your reader. How can you persuade a reader with your story? How might you get readers to identify with your protagonist? What argument might your story implicitly make?
- Personal essay: Using "Eleven" as an idea generator, write about a time you had a positive or negative experience in school. What lesson did you learn that day? Help your reader understand the benefit or harm in your situation.
- Social argument: "Eleven" raises problems with the power relations in the average K-12 classroom. What should be done to ensure that students have voices or that teachers are prepared to use their power to good ends?
- Comic: Create a short comic (either strip or short story) of any of the above or a different idea of your own. Use visuals and text in combination to draw an emotional and intellectual response from your readers.

Of course, this approach can be utilized with any short story. Mitch usually repeats the lesson with at least one or two other stories over the course of the unit, and he mixes contemporary works like Cisneros' with classics like James Joyce's "Araby" or Kate Chopin's "The Story of an Hour." When students use storytelling techniques in other essays they write, those essays will come alive with human anecdotes that illustrate the students' messages.

THE STANDARDS HAVE ROOM FOR FICTION

There is genre variety in the aforementioned writing prompts, but all of those invitations lead students to creative forms that still illustrate an argument. The pieces—especially the personal essays or short stories—would not look like traditional essays. The argument itself may be implied rather than stated, but it would still defend a claim. Writings like this would also put a name and face to the issue.

Linda Rief said, "Arguments start with story" (2015), but the CCSS put more focus on argumentation than narration. It is vital that teachers don't ignore the fact that the two overlap. Any standards document, including the CCSS, has to oversimplify matters in an attempt to fit cognitive work into tidy categories. That is not how our brains work, though. Our brains are powerful and don't always need to keep thoughts in bullet points and subcategories. We mix narration, information, and argumentation all the time. The curriculum must respect that, and student learning can only benefit by taking advantage of these natural mental overlaps.

In isolation, a student's story might be considered more persuasion than argumentation, but the skills learned can easily be applied the next time the student writes an academic paper. Lively arguments include anecdotes and descriptions as evidence. These are rhetorical elements students gain from reading good fiction. People gain writing skills from seeing them used, so teachers must continue to use fiction in the classroom, even if the course is focused solely on essay writing. Our brains think in narrative. Our very lives are stories. Our essays will improve if we bring good storytelling techniques found in fiction to our nonfiction too.

PERSONALIZED LITERARY ANALYSIS

In "On Essaying," James Moffett writes that the essay should be "a candid blend of personal and universal," and that "what we really want to help youngsters learn is how to express ideas of universal value in a personal voice" (1987).

Moffett's words, themselves part of a personal piece that might be called an "essay," capture what so many of us have struggled with as English teachers: we don't want to read lifeless, limp prose that recycles the same formulaic ideas in the same formulaic patterns that we've seen before, and we don't want students to write that prose, that prose that, in all probability, they've likewise written before. Arguably, the world doesn't need another five-paragraph essay on *The Great Gatsby*. It doesn't need another five-paragraph argument that Jay Gatsby is (or is not) a tragic hero; it doesn't need another formulaic argument that Fitzgerald believes that the wealthy are selfish, arrogant, and careless.

That said, that novel—like any work of art—is still worthy of academic and artistic exploration. Why?

- We want students to continue to develop their analytical and close-reading skills. Writing about literature is *one* way to do this.
- We want students to probe deeply into texts, exploring the ideas and questions that authors raise and reacting to them. Writing about literature is *one* way to do this.
- We want students to continue to develop their organizational and compositional skills. Writing about literature is *one* way to do this.

What Dirk has realized, in his high school English classes, is that he needs to ask whether the assignments that he gives are pushing students toward these goals or whether those assignments are asking students to recycle ideas, formulas, and the same tired prose that they've written before.

One way that teachers can encourage a less formulaic, but potentially more powerful, response to literature is to first seek a personal connection with the work in question. As Romano writes in *Clearing the Way* (1987), "When students write essays in my classes, I urge them to discover personal links with the literature and to let that guide them in choosing the topic and focus of their papers. I help them learn to do this by demonstrating through my own writing and storytelling how I have made personal links with literature" (150).

In his 11th and 12th grade English classes, Dirk encourages students to find within any given work a topic or a question that is of particular personal importance and build an essay or a paper around that. One AP English Language and Composition student, after reading *The Brothers Karamazov*, found her belief in a traditional notion of God shaken and wrote a strong paper exploring both how that happened and how Dostoyevsky explored that same doubt. Another student, in an English 11 Honors class, felt that she truly understood *Of Mice and Men* only after writing an essay that discussed her relationship with her older sister, who had just left for her first year of college.

Another student in AP English Language and Composition wrote a lengthy paper on *Moby Dick* and his grandfather's recent death. Using a personal narrative as the frame for his exploration of Melville's text, Aaron discussed how both Ahab and he found themselves rubbing against the seemingly unanswerable questions of the universe. In the narrative essay, excerpts of which are shown in Figure 5.2, Aaron manipulates much of the same imagery as Melville as he struggles to punch through his own series of pasteboard masks.

It's possible that Aaron could have come to as profound an understanding of Melville's novel in a formulaic essay arguing why Ahab *really* wants to kill

Excerpt from paper:	Conclusion to paper:
As we strolled slowly, [my father] asked if I wanted to talk about anything. I did, but my mouth stayed closed. We walked back through the white corridor, past the heroic murals, the cafeteria and out into the parking garage. I looked at my watch. My dad and I were still quiet until this point. Then I responded to his inquiry, 'It's funny,' I began, I keep looking at my watch, and the second hand doesn't stop moving.' My dad stopped walking. 'These are [my grandfather's] last minutes,' I continued, 'but in our lives, this amount of time is the sound of a pin dropped near a jet engine.' I had made the realizations as I spoke. 'In the scheme of time, what is this?' I asked my dad. These moments were most precious, but what was lost were those I had failed to notice as precious—as all moments are. As that very moment was. My dad recognized my youth, and smiled. Even I knew there was still so much to learn—and I wanted to know it all. Why do we die? Why are good people taken from us? Those pictures on the walls didn't show the truth—people dying; it's something we all do. I was angry.	*Ahab's questions could never be answered, but there is nothing wrong with asking those questions—it gives life purpose—but Melville warns his readers of what can happen when these questions are taken too far. We are not whales, and we can't charge at one and not expect to get hurt. We cannot ask unanswerable questions and expect immortal answers. We are only human and are governed by the laws of Nature—or god, or fate, or whatever one may call it. Try as we may—and as a society we have the uncanny ability to try—we will never be able to answer these questions. We will never be able to stop asking them though—and will always attempt to understand.*

Figure 5.2   Excerpts from a student's AP English Language and Composition paper on *Moby Dick*

the whale, but it is far from certain. What Aaron discovered as he wrote about his grandfather, as he explored his ongoing reaction to his family's loss, was not only the personal relevance of Ahab's quest, but also how to express one of the many specific arguments that Melville makes in that novel. As Dirk has discovered in his classroom, personal narratives are one way to approach analytical writing, but, sometimes, students don't need to narrate their lives so much as they might need to narrate their experiences of reading a given text. Tal, a high school senior, wrote about his response to Kurt Vonnegut's *Slaughterhouse-Five* and, by engaging in the reflection, came to a conclusion of what he thought the book was really about (see Figure 5.3).

Of course, having a reaction to a novel, play, or poem may not be enough in and of itself. Teachers may need students to transform an initial reaction (often expressed as "this is what I felt" or "this is what I thought about") into a more measured consideration of the nature of that work. Early on in Dirk's English courses, whether "regular," "honors," or "Advanced Placement," he tries to encourage students to see every work they read as making an argument.

When his English 11 students look at Sharon Olds' poem, "The Possessive," for example, they consider, along with their evolving reactions to its content, the argument it seems to make. Instead of discussing it as being simply "about growing up" or "about mothers and daughters," the students try to find their way to a specific argument that the poem makes about this particular relationship. In that argument (say, perhaps, something like, "The speaker of the poem views the daughter's haircut as a violent act of rebellion"), they can find a "universal" meaning, or theme.

I realized Vonnegut is absolutely correct in his idea that people should 'never do nothing.' The human question 'why me?' is important in that it asserts us as individuals who think on our own and search for answers to questions that arise from our experiences. Billy Pilgrim used his travels to Tralfamadore, and his belief that there is no free will, as a coping method for the things he'd seen in war, such as the bombing of Dresden. This coping method is too similar to real life in that people make excuses for, or simply convince themselves, that there is nothing they can do in a given situation. Of course, believing one can do nothing is satisfying because it is equivalent to having done everything possible—there are no further steps to take. I came away from Slaughterhouse-Five understanding how Vonnegut wants readers to understand the choices they make always have consequences, and doing nothing like Billy Pilgrim is what contributes to atrocities like the Dresden bombing. Many people, including me before reading this novel, don't consider coping methods such as ignorance, fate, or determinism as negative things.

Figure 5.3 A student's response to Kurt Vonnegut's *Slaughterhouse-Five*

Just as Sharon Olds—or other great writers from Ernest Hemingway to Toni Morrison to William Shakespeare—might make an argument in a creative work, students can likewise argue a specific understanding of a work of art, or their lives, or the world around them, in any number of ways. All too often, we remember to ask students to read a variety of genres and styles but ask them to write, in response to that wide variety of works, only in one specific form. If we remind ourselves, though, of our reasons for having students read and respond to literature, we quickly see that simplistic responses—whether multiple-choice "objective tests" or formulaic papers—do not necessarily allow our students to achieve our goals:

- We want students to engage with texts on a level that goes beyond knowing the facts of the plot.
- We want students to think about the issues and questions raised in the texts and how the author raises them.
- We want students to consider issues of character, within the texts and within themselves.
- We want students to connect texts with others they've read and to track common themes, personal connections, and their (potentially) changing opinions.
- We want students to feel like they can contribute to an ongoing interaction between a society of readers and the texts it has chosen.
- We want students to make leaps from seeing the broad questions that a novel can raise to asking those questions of themselves and actively seeking the answers.

As we have observed in our classrooms, multiple-choice tests and simplistic responses to binary questions like, "Is Macbeth a tragic hero?" generally fail to achieve those goals. Likewise, nothing in those goals dictates a formulaic response to any one particular work of art.

One student—as Andrew did in one of Dirk's English 12 Honors classes—might express his understanding of Cormac McCarthy's *The Road* as if it were a lost episode of *My Little Pony* and discover within that framework the freedom to explore the nature and importance of love, kindness, and humanity in a world seemingly devoid of beauty and hope.

Another student might reach a deeper understanding of Toni Morrison's *Beloved* by writing a letter about self-definition to a future son or daughter, where another might decide to mirror *The Grapes of Wrath* and compose an analytical paper interrupted by intercalary paragraphs reflecting on the presence (or absence) of empathy, love, and humanity within his own high school.

There are still significant, particular, and profound challenges in helping high school and college students write analytically about literature. One such challenge is, of course, weaning students of the easy-out of the five-paragraph argument and convincing them, through this weaning, that analysis does not necessarily mean simple "proof" of a simple claim. Another is helping students find that they—as readers, as writers, as thinkers—have valid insights and opinions about the fundamental questions that literature raises, and that true analysis often involves taking risky positions or considering risky or uncertain arguments. Finally, it is difficult to help students present their analyses in clean, clear, insightful, concrete, and specific language.

Students—as readers, as writers, as thinkers— have valid insights and opinions about the fundamental questions that literature raises, and true analysis often involves taking risky positions or considering risky or uncertain arguments.

POETRY AND ARGUMENT

In order to meet this last challenge, Dirk has found it helpful to have his students read and write a great deal of poetry in his English classrooms. The best analytical writing (and, arguably, the best writing, *period*) is concise, precise, and specific. It does not deal in generalities. It has no patience for vague language or insubstantial claims. It is, in other words, quite similar to the best poetry.

As we read poetry in our English classes, we try to spend time not only on what poetry does (or tries to do), but also what it consciously tries to avoid:

The vague. Give the specifics, always. *Thing* is vague. *Mammal* is a little better. *Elephant* gives me something I can see. *Bull elephant pacing his cage* offers a bit more yet. *Sound* doesn't tell me much. *City sound* is still pretty open. *Traffic* is, perhaps, clearer. *Friday afternoon traffic* lets me see, hear, and smell an image (and makes me tense, too). *I miss my ex-girlfriend* is so general as to be meaningless. *My tan-line from your class ring reminds me only that you're gone* is a step in a more specific, meaningful direction.

The cliché. We don't read clichés. We don't really see clichés. Or, at least, we no longer see the individual parts of a cliché. We skip past them quickly, without thought, without sight, without feel—and that's a dangerous reader reaction. If clichés are, as George Orwell said, dying metaphors, then they have taken what was once effective, vivid language and transformed it into that which is empty and bland.

Hackneyed language. Like a cliché, a bit of hackneyed language is a combination of words that no longer exist as independent parts and no longer carry any particular weight. We don't see *radiant smiles,* or *crashing waves,* or feel a *tender touch,* or hear a *rumble of thunder,* or know who *the American People* are. We don't even really *question authority* when we see it on a bumper sticker.

Broad generalities. It's a tough lesson for all writers: giant, unfocused lumps of generality don't offer any specific meaning to readers. Overused abstractions—love, death, patriotism, fear, pride, nature, and sin—are too broad for meaning. "A great feeling of patriotism welled in my chest" doesn't tell your poem's reader anything about *how* you actually felt.

You can see the same effect with vague, ultimately meaningless thesis statements like, "Hemingway's language is very effective" or "Fitzgerald criticizes the wealthy" or "Shakespeare thinks young lovers are foolish." Poetry won't settle for such broad generalities; neither should analytical writing.

There are a variety of lessons that teachers can use to help students recognize that what makes the best poetry (like the best examples of any genre of literature) work is its attention to detail and its refusal to compromise the specific for the vague. One that Dirk has had success with it is taking any relatively "traditional" analytical prompt and having students compose not an "essay" but a poem in response to it. The poem, then, must not only address the prompt (say, for example, the relationship of Bromden's childhood to his experience in Nurse Ratched's ward in Ken Kesey's *One Flew Over the Cuckoo's Nest*), but also work according to the standards a class can generate for evaluating poetry: specific, concrete, powerful, utilizing the best possible language, and so on.

Another option is to have students take a part of a rough draft of an analytical paper (no matter what form that draft might take) and convert it into poetry. In converting it, they can eliminate whatever words they want, but cannot add any. Seen as a poem, an introduction that simply praises an author's craft or that begins to argue that a work as complex as *King Lear* merely "presents important lessons for any family" might appear more obviously in need of further revision.

Perhaps, after such work, students might rework the language of an introduction. Perhaps, they might rework the very claims of that introduction. Perhaps, like Julia, a student in Dirk's AP English Literature and Composition class, they might rework the entire framework of a paper so that, instead of a vague assertion of the "many important themes of Ann Patchet's *Bel Canto*," her introduction could read,

A woman sits quietly in the back of an open ambulance, her eyes strained, her voice hoarse. In the midst of the rushed officials and overbearing medics, she is alone in her mind, thinking repeatedly of one question: Why do these bad things happen to good people? Tired, she listens to the stunned silence heard only after a fall.

Her name is Roxanne Coss. She is, and once was, a singer. She is small and short, she hails from Chicago, and once, she was held at gunpoint.

Certainly, Julia might have arrived at that introduction through "traditional" methods of in-class revision (teacher feedback, peer-based writing groups, etc.), but, in this case, working with poetry helped her see that over-generalized assertions only weakened her case and that the more specific and concrete she made her claims, the stronger her argument became.

IN SHORT

- The CCSS say students should read 70 percent nonfiction and 30 percent fiction over the course of one school day, which has led many English teachers to cut some fiction. Upon closer analysis, though, if anything, English teachers should be using *more* fiction to meet this suggestion.
- Creativity is not limited to "creative writing." Essays, academic, and informational writing all benefit from creative techniques like storytelling.
- Going beyond the old school essay affects reading choices too.
- Picture books provide an accessible and engaging way to analyze the rhetorical choices writers make.
- Short fiction works well for helping students see how stories, and not just essays, are arguments.
- Inviting students to write creatively can lead to deeper, more personal and personally meaningful literary analysis.
- The reading and writing of poetry supports student learning and improves specificity in student writing.

Chapter 6

The Real Work

The first time I confronted the five-paragraph essay, I lost. It wasn't even close. During my senior year of high school, I took AP English Language and Composition, taught by the same man who had taught my sophomore literature class, opened me up to the possibility that I might have something to say about writers and their works, and invited me to serve on the school newspaper.

Although I began the year full of argument, Marxism, rebellion, and poised on the edge of a very short editorial fuse, I found myself, by the middle of winter, ready to spend some time thinking and writing, rather than arguing and writing. I was, I must admit, tired of debates, tired of argument, tired of shouting. I was ready for nuance. I was reading more, discovering Socratic dialogue through old books of my grandfather, losing myself in the endless spiritual explorations of Dostoyevsky, and falling hard for the complex magic of Garcia-Marquez. I was ready, finally, for nuance.

That winter, my teacher assigned a paper. We were, he said, to find a controversial topic of interest and write a persuasive essay about it. While I do not, I confess, remember the exact details of the assignment, I know that we needed to have a thesis, a central point around which we could construct our essay. I know, too, that I felt ready. My work on the newspaper had introduced me to the columns of writers like Mike Royko, showing me the wild diversity of forms with which a person could construct an argument.

I had no problem choosing my issue. I wanted to write about the War on Drugs. I did not, however, want to spend only five paragraphs arguing the issue. I did not end my introduction with a statement akin to, "Drugs should be legalized because . . ." and conclude my paper with a slightly expanded version of the same sentence. I did not want to wrap an explicit thesis statement around three key points, each with a morsel of evidence or two to make it convincing. I did not want to be obvious. I wanted to work with figurative language and vignettes. I wanted to manipulate the elements of language the way that the writers I was coming to admire did. I wanted to write something real, something meaningful, and something good.

On the day the essays were due, I handed my teacher the product of two weeks' thinking, writing, researching, considering, and rewriting. At that time, it was odd enough for me to begin a paper more than twelve hours before it was due. Odder still for me to revise or rewrite. I did both for this paper.

It was, I felt confident, the best thing I had ever written.

I was accustomed to receiving decent grades on written assignments, even when I had put little work into them. I worked my butt off for this one; surely, I would be rewarded.

My teacher gave it a C. My content, he said, was reasonably good, but the essay did not follow "the form."

My first paragraph did not include my three main points of evidence. I used fragments. I composed a paragraph of a single sentence, a short rhetorical question standing alone between long bouts of constitutional and legal philosophy.

I didn't have three middle paragraphs of five to seven sentences, each paragraph with a single opinion justified by at least two pieces of evidence. Instead, I had arguments, counterarguments, rationalizations, analogies, testimonials, discussion, vignettes, and analysis. I had what felt to me like a thorough consideration of the issue and a conclusion that actually took into account the content of the whole paper, not simply what I might have said in the introduction.

I also had, however, more than five paragraphs. Oops.

The grade I received might not have affected me much if I had not come to care so much about that paper. But it did. And it took me until my freshman year of college to unlearn what it taught me about how to write an "essay," when a professor returned an early composition with this comment: "An acceptable paper, but one in which the writer has worked well within his limits. Part of the challenge in assigned papers is to find ways of making topics personally meaningful and important. I expect to see more life in your writing/thinking than this paper displays."

—Dirk

So how do we make this all happen? How can we help our students display "more life in [their] writing/thinking?" In isolation, any one of the suggestions made in this book will improve the quality of your students' learning. But we can't stop there. Updating how we teach reading and writing takes more than a couple of tweaks to lesson plans. It asks us to re-evaluate our practice.

SHIFTING THE FOCUS

This book is ultimately about shifting our approach, which will take more than just sliding in a new visual literacy activity or introducing better variety in our classroom texts. It's not as much about modifying our curriculum as it is about modifying our mind-set. Below, we outline several suggestions for incorporating more complex, creative, authentic, and contemporary experiences into an existing curriculum. But if we're merely plugging in new assignments, we're not getting the job done.

Somewhere between inputting grades and administering standardized tests, we often lose sight of our ultimate course objectives. What is it that we want our students to learn in our classes? When asked what we teach in American Literature, teachers often respond with *The Scarlet Letter* or *The Adventures of Huckleberry Finn*. That's wrong—or at least it should be. If we're simply teaching a text, we're missing the point. *Huck Finn* is a vehicle that allows us to teach the skills and understandings we hope our students gain in American Literature. *Huck Finn* cannot be our course objective. When asked what we teach in American Literature, we should respond with a learning objective, or at least have one in mind:

> This book is ultimately about shifting our approach. It's not as much about modifying our curriculum as it is about modifying our mindset.

- "This is the year we help students leave behind the five-paragraph essay in favor of more complex writing."
- "In this course, students learn to analyze and produce texts advocating for social change."
- "Students will be able to read and write their world through analysis of contemporary and historical, traditional and multimodal texts."
- "By the end of this class, students will have learned to engage in authentic, real-world writing for a genuine audience."

Ultimately, students need to *think*. If our final exams are asking students to merely recall characters in *The Great Gatsby*, we aren't assessing their growth at all—and we certainly aren't assessing their ability to think. Likewise, if we are expecting a simple for/against, five-paragraph essay in response to a contemporary text, we have gained little. Or, if students are participating in "discourse" activities by merely stating and restating a claim, they have avoided critical thinking.

If we want our students to truly grow through exposure to contemporary texts, real-world complexity, civic discourse, multimodal sources, and creativity, we need to emphasize the critical thinking and the learning process over the grades and the final product.

ASSESSING FOR THINKING

How we assess student writing is as important as how we teach writing. Teacher feedback, whether in the form of written comments, circles on a rubric, or a letter grade, tells students what to value and where to focus their energy in the future. If we want our students to write complex, sophisticated arguments, we need to make sure our feedback indicates this.

> How we assess student writing is as important as how we teach writing. Teacher feedback, whether in the form of written comments, circles on a rubric, or a letter grade, tells students what to value and where to focus their energy in the future.

The authors of this book prefer a holistic approach to assessing student writing, as non-holistic assessment tends to reward formulaic writing. If students are working with a checklist of items such as "clear thesis statement" and "transitions between paragraphs," teachers end up reading a lot of simplistic writing that is compliant but vacuous. In her book *Rethinking Rubrics in Writing Assessment* (2006), Maja Wilson explains that when teachers use a rubric to assess an essay that does not follow the five-paragraph formula, they "score it more harshly" and "provide feedback in a way that will only force the writer to rewrite in five-paragraph essay format" (p. 39). This is precisely what we want to avoid with our writing assessment.

Using these highly specific rubric grids is understandable: it makes grading easier, and it gives students simple feedback and justification for a grade. But if our goal is to help develop quality writers and thinkers, we need to provide feedback that more clearly appreciates the complex nature of writing. Good essays, such as Dirk's high school essay, described in the vignette at the beginning of this chapter, are not always rewarded with highly specific rubrics, but mediocre writing, in contrast, often scores quite well.

Instead of relying on overly simple methods of assessing student writing, we need to trust ourselves to identify good writing. Holistic grading can take into account that which is not easily measured: the nuances of the argument, the student's voice, the critical thinking made visible, the creativity in expressing a position.

Even the scoring criteria used to assess writing on Advanced Placement exams, the SAT, and the ACT are holistic in nature and encourage complex thought. The College Board's scoring guide for the SAT essay, for example, rewards essays that "insightfully [develop] a point of view" and "[demonstrate] outstanding critical thinking." There is no mention of, let alone check box for, a thesis statement in the description of a "typical" top-scoring essay (College Board 2015). And although the specifics of the AP English Language and Composition Scoring Guidelines change from year to year, the scoring guidelines always remind readers to "[make] certain to reward students for what they do well," and the highest scoring responses are described as being "especially sophisticated in their argument" (College Board 2010).

We can also facilitate better writing and thinking in our classroom when we start to value process over product. If we only grade the final paper, we aren't considering what the writer did to arrive at that final product. Dirk's experience as a student in AP English Language and Composition demonstrates the danger of ignoring the writing process. Kelly Gallagher, author of several books on the teaching of writing, sometimes goes so far as to skip grading final drafts altogether and instead "only grade the movement between drafts" in order to encourage thoughtful revision (Gallagher 2012). The writing process is where the thinking occurs, and we cannot afford to ignore that which we hope to promote.

Revision, unfortunately, can be difficult to meaningfully assess. Today, however, newer technologies such as Google Docs are increasingly available in K-12 classrooms. When a student "shares" a document with her teacher, the student provides the teacher with access to her writing process (and thereby much of her thinking); the teacher can watch the student write and can view the changes that are made each time the student sits down at a computer.

Teachers who don't have access to this or similar technology can still shift their assessment to value the writing process. Many years ago, before the ubiquity of student devices, Carrie taught an essay writing class in which all students' final papers received As—providing the students continued to revise and rework their papers until they were the best they could be. The stack of drafts stapled in the upper left-hand corner became a point of proud exasperation for many students: "Look how many drafts I've done!" Once the teacher and the students get used to this new mind-set and value process over product, then the learning begins to flourish.

Regardless of how we go about doing it, it is essential that our assessment aligns with our ultimate goals. Learning should be valued over grades, and our feedback should be as thoughtful as we expect our students' writing to be. Also, we need to remember that reflective conversation with a student about his or her writing will lead to more growth than any letter or number ever can.

STARTING SMALL

It's easy to feel overwhelmed when designing instruction. As teachers, we are trying to meet the standards handed down to us by politicians; we are trying to follow the curriculum established by our school districts; we are trying to implement the strategies introduced at our latest professional development session; we are trying to engage and respond to the needs of our students. The list could go on, but the point is that teachers have many stakeholders to please and demands to meet, all while trying to remain true to what they know is pedagogically sound and effective practice.

> The good news is that the teaching practices outlined in this book don't require you to abandon your existing curriculum. Rather, once teachers have bought into the underlying shift in pedagogical focus, there are several simple steps we can take to act within the framework of our existing curricula.

The good news is that the teaching practices outlined in this book don't require you to abandon your existing curriculum. Teachers need not scrap what they have been doing, and, of course, in most districts they would not be allowed to do so anyway. Rather, once teachers have bought into the underlying shift in pedagogical focus, there are several simple steps we can take to act within the framework of our existing curricula.

Incorporating Contemporary Texts

The authors of this book aren't advocating an uprising against the anthologized essay. The classic essays of Emerson, Orwell, and Thoreau (among others) have endured for good reasons. Instead of renouncing these texts, teachers must simply consider current texts to supplement the curriculum. If we fail to include current texts, students may come to see formal writing as an antiquated means of expression, and they will miss out on opportunities to become proficient at reading and analyzing contemporary language, syntax, and style.

Additionally, teachers must consider the more subtle messages they send by the texts they choose. Anthologized writers tend to be less racially, ethnically, and sexually diverse than those featured in the latest edition of *The Atlantic* or *The New Yorker*, and because of historical power and opportunity gaps, the older the anthology, the more severe the disparity. If the vast majority of our classroom texts are authored by White men, we're inadvertently telling many of our students that people *like them* haven't made valuable contributions to the field of writing. Again, this doesn't mean we shouldn't teach from our textbooks; it means that we shouldn't teach from *only* our textbooks.

If our entire curriculum includes texts that are at least half a century old, we also run the risk of suggesting that past issues are irrelevant to the present. For example, we love teaching Martin Luther King, Jr.'s, "Letter from Birmingham Jail," but if we fail to pair it with a recent text, we implicitly suggest that racial inequity is a thing of the past. So, yes, continue to teach the eloquent writing of Martin Luther King Jr., but teach it alongside Jelani Cobb or Ta-Nehisi Coates.

Keeping It Real

In the "real world," argument has a real audience and a real purpose. Many of our existing writing assignments only need to be tweaked for students to make the shift from writing for the teacher and for the grade to writing for more authentic audiences and purposes. In addition to the ideas shared in chapter 3, there are several small shifts that can help make students' experience more authentic and engaging—and, often, students' arguments will naturally become more complex as they strive to reach a wider audience.

Consider simple ways to publish student work. That independent reading book report? Make it a book review, and have students share it on GoodReads, Amazon, or a class website that current and future students can browse and comment on. When you assign an essay in response to a novel, help students identify real audiences for their chosen topics: Is it intended for the author or publisher? Somebody who could benefit from the book's message? The committee responsible for including the book in the curriculum? Students can reframe their essay as a letter while still practicing all of the essential writing traits we want them to master. It's amazing how much more pride students take in work that will be available to a wider audience.

Making Room for Creativity

Good writing *is* creative, even in essay form. But we can encourage even more creativity if we, as teachers, are more creative in our approach to literacy instruction.

As secondary and postsecondary educators have moved away from traditional creative endeavors, the business world has increasingly sought creativity in its employees. In fact, creativity is widely valued as the most important trait for future leaders in the corporate world (Tomasco 2010). It makes sense, then, as we strive to prepare our students for the future, that we embrace creativity in our classrooms. Any student can be taught to write an analytical essay, but to add another layer—a creative presentation of that analysis, for example—requires students to exercise their minds in new ways. Creative responses require students to think in more critical, more complex ways.

It's easy for teachers to fall into the routine of giving tests and assigning essays simply because that's the convention. If we stop to consider exactly *what* we want to assess, however, we open up a world of possibilities.

Are you interested in learning whether the student understood the major themes of a novel? Ask students to write a poem, create a picture book, or build a website exploring a theme. Do you want to make sure students understand characterization? Ask them to draw and label a character portrait or to blog from a character's perspective. These assignments are actually more complex—but also more fun—than teaching with only traditional tests and essays because they ask students to think both creatively and analytically.

FINAL THOUGHT

In order to help our students read, write, and think more critically, we must move beyond the anthologized essay and the simplistic argument. There is great value in many of school's traditional practices, but it's okay to admit much of what we do needs updating. The world beyond the school doors does not function like a textbook. It does not fit into neat formulas or tidy packages. It probably never did, but as society progresses, it—like life itself—only grows more complex.

When we allow students to engage with contemporary readings and issues, we acknowledge that students already live in the real world. This is perhaps the most important mind-set shift we can make as teachers. Why? Why must we invite the real world into the classroom? Why must we ask students to grapple with the hard work of twenty-first-century life? Why must we allow the disorganized, sloppy world into our well-planned, thoughtful lessons?

That answer is simple: It is ultimately our job to help prepare our students to run that very real world. That world is a little messy, but our students are up to the task. Let's let them do real work.

References

American Dialect Society. (2006). "Truthiness voted 2005 word of the year." *American Dialect Society.* Retrieved from http://www.americandialect.org/.

Atwell, N. (1998). *In the Middle* (2nd ed.). Portsmouth, NH: Heinemann.

Bakhtin, M. M. and Holquist, M. (1982). *The Dialogic Imagination: Four Essays.* Austin, TX: University of Texas Press.

Beane, J. (1997). *Curriculum Integration: Designing the Core of Democratic Education.* New York: Teachers College Press, Columbia University.

Beers, K. (2002). *When Kids Can't Read: When Teachers Can Do.* Portsmouth, NH: Heinemann.

Bernan, K., Boulton, I., Eidman-Aadahl, E., Fleming, J., Gardner, L., Rogers, I., and Solomon, A. (Eds.) (2006). *Writing for a Change.* San Francisco, CA: Jossey-Bass.

Block, A. B. (February 9, 2012). "5 questions with George Lucas: Controversial 'Star Wars' changes, sopa, and 'Indiana Jones 5'." *The Hollywood Reporter.* Retrieved from http://www.hollywoodreporter.com/heat-vision/george-lucas-star-wars-interview-288523.

Bomer, R. and Bomer, K. (2001). *For a Better World: Reading and Writing for Social Action.* Portsmouth, NH: Heinemann.

Borsheim, C. and Petrone, R. (2006). "Teaching the research paper for local action." *English Journal,* 95(4), 78–83.

Brekke, K. (May 5, 2014). "Sarah McLachlan: 'I change the channel' when my ASPCA commercials come on." *HuffPost Live.* Retrieved from http://www.huffingtonpost.com/2014/05/05/sarah-mclachlan-aspca_n_5267840.html.

Burke, J. (2010). *What's the Big Idea? Question-driven Units to Motivate Reading, Writing, and Thinking.* Portsmouth, NH: Heinemann.

Burke, K. (1973). *The Philosophy of Literary Form: Studies in Symbolic Action* (3rd ed.). Berkeley: University of California Press.

Campbell, K. H. (2010). "Eavesdropping on contemporary minds: Why we need more essays in our high school classrooms." *English Journal,* 99(4), 50–54.

Cillizza, C. (2013). "Worst. Congress. Ever. The case in 7 charts." *The Washington Post*. Retrieved from https://www.washingtonpost.com/news/the-fix/wp/2013/10/31/worst-congress-ever-the-case-in-7-charts/.

Cisneros, S. (1992). *Woman Hollering Creek*. New York, NY: Vintage Books.

Coates, T. (2015). "Take down the Confederate flag—Now." *The Atlantic*. Retrieved from http://www.theatlantic.com/politics/archive/2015/06/take-down-the-confederate-flag-now/396290/.

Cohen, D. S. (Writer) and Dietter, S. (Director). (1996). "Much apu about nothing [Televison series episode]." In G. Daniels and G. Meyer (executive producers), *The Simpsons*. Los Angeles, CA: Fox.

College Board. (2010). "AP English language and composition 2010 scoring guidelines." *AP Central*. Retrieved October 31, 2015, from http://apcentral.collegeboard.com/apc/public/repository/ap10_english_language_scoring_guidelines.pdf.

College Board. (n.d.). "Essay scoring." *SAT*. Retrieved October 31, 2015, from https://sat.collegeboard.org/scores/sat-essay-scoring-guide.

Common Core State Standards Initiative. (2015). English language arts standards. Retrieved from http://www.corestandards.org/ELA-Literacy/.

Digital Is. (n.d.). Retrieved from digitalis.nwp.org.

Dillard, A. (1985). "Transfiguration." *The Norton Sampler*. New York, NY: W.W. Norton & Company, Inc.

Drysdale, E., Gwinn, P., Katsir, J., and Krafft, L. (Writers) and Hoskinson, J. (Director). (2005). "Stone Phillips [Television series episode]." In S. Colbert (executive producer), *The Colbert Report*. New York, NY: Comedy Central.

Dr. Seuss. (1971). *The Lorax*. New York, NY: Random House.

Dr. Seuss. (1984). *The Butter Battle Book*. New York, NY: Random House.

Dubus, A., III. (May 18, 2012). "Writing inspiration from Andre Dubus III: How to stay true to yourself." *Writer's Digest*. Retrieved from http://www.writersdigest.com/editor-blogs/there-are-no-rules/writing-inspiration-from-andre-dubus-iii-how-to-stay-true-to-yourself.

Frederickson, G., Roos, F. (Producers), and Coppola, F. F. (Director). (2005). *The Outsiders: The Complete Novel [Motion Picture]*. United States: Warner Bros. Pictures.

Fulwiler, T. (1997). *College Writing: A Personal Approach to Academic Writing* (2nd ed.). Portsmouth, NH: Boynton/Cook.

Gallagher, K. [KellyGToGo]. (February 14, 2012). Sometimes I don't grade the final drafts. Sometimes I only grade the movement between drafts. This encourages all to revise meaningfully [Tweet]. Retrieved from https://twitter.com/KellyGToGo/status/169599513743458304.

Gallagher, K. (2015). *In the Best Interest of Students: Staying True to What Works in the ELA Classroom*. Portland, ME: Stenhouse.

Garcia, A. (Ed.). (2014). *Teaching in the Connected Learning Classroom: The Digital Media & Learning Research Hub Report Series on Connected Learning*. Retrieved from http://www.nwp.org/cs/public/download/nwp_file/19025/teaching_in_the_CL_classroom.pdf?x-r=pcfile_d.

Gerber, S. [SabraGerber]. (February 24, 2015). "You're in high school, people ask, 'What do you want to be?' This question sucks. It ignores everything that you already are." #ww21 #and. [Tweet]. Retrieved from https://twitter.com/SabraGerber/status/570258981924540416.

Gladwell, M. (2008). *Outliers*. Boston, MA: Little, Brown and Company.

Gladwell, M. (2009). "The courthouse ring." *The New Yorker*. Retrieved from http://www.newyorker.com/magazine/2009/08/10/the-courthouse-ring.

Greene, M. (1978). *Landscapes of Learning*. New York, NY: Teachers College Press.

Hillocks, G. (2011). *Teaching Argument Writing, Grades 6–12: Supporting Claims with Relevant Evidence and Clear Reasoning*. Portsmouth, NH: Boynton/Cook.

Homan, E. C. and Reed, D. (2014). "Learning from digital students and teachers: Reimagining writing instruction and assessment for the 21st century." In R. McClure and J. Purdy (Eds.), *The Next Digital Scholar: A Fresh Approach to the Common Core State Standards in Research and Writing* (pp. 35–67). Medford, NJ: Information Today, Inc.

Humans of New York. (n.d.). Retrieved from http://www.humansofnewyork.com/

Ito, M., Gutiérrez, K. D., Livingstone, S., Penuel, B., Rhodes, J., Salen, K., . . . Watkins, S. C. (2013). Connected learning: An agenda for research and design. Retrieved from http://clrn.dmlhub.net/publications/connected-learning-an-agenda-for-research-and-design.

Jenkins, H. and Kelley, W. (2013). *Reading in a Participatory Culture: Remixing Moby-Dick in the English Classroom*. New York, NY: Teachers College Press.

Juzwik, M., Borsheim-Black, C., Caughlan, S., and Heintz, A. (2013). *Inspiring Dialogue: Talking to Learn in the English Classroom*. New York: Teachers College Press.

KQED. (n.d.). About KQED. Retrieved from http://www.kqed.org/about/.

King, S. (2004). *The Dark Tower*. Hampton Falls, NH: Donald M. Grant, Publisher.

Kittle, P. (2012). *Book Love*. Portsmouth, NH: Heinemann.

Kittle, P. [pennykittle]. (February 24, 2015). "Arguments start with story." @ LindaMRief #PacLit15 I've truly never seen kids write so well so fast as they do with Linda's wise guidance. [Tweet]. Retrieved from https://twitter.com/pennykittle/status/628225805311586304.

Kolbert, E. (September 5, 2013). "Have sports teams brought down America's schools?" *The New Yorker*. Retrieved from http://www.newyorker.com/news/daily-comment/have-sports-teams-brought-down-americas-schools.

Krashen, S. (2004). *The Power of Reading*. Santa Barbara, CA: Libraries Unlimited.

Lerman, K. (2001). "In favor of Napster." *Writing!*, 23(4), 15.

Mahajan, K. (October 21, 2015). "The two Asian Americas [Review of the book *The Making of Asian America*]." *The New Yorker*. Retrieved from http://www.newyorker.com/books/page-turner/the-two-asian-americas.

Mar, R. and Oatley, K. (2008). "The function of fiction is the abstraction and simulation of social experience." *Perspectives on Psychological Science*, 3(3), 173–92.

Marchetti, A. and O'Dell, R. (2015). *Writing with Mentors*. Portsmouth, NH: Heinemann.

McLachlan, S. (1997). "Angel." On *Surfacing* [CD]. New York City, NY: Arista Records.

Mencken, H. L. (1982). *A Mencken Chrestomathy: His Own Selection of His Choicest Writing*. New York, NY: Vintage Books.

Merriam-Webster. (2006). "2006 word of the year." *Merriam-Webster.* Retrieved from http://www.merriam-webster.com/word-of-the-year/2006-word-of-the-year. htm.

Miller, M. (August 27, 2014). *Dispelling the Myth of the Standardized Writing Test.* Lecture presented at Fairfax County Public Schools High School English In-Service General Session and CLT Collaboration at Fairfax High School, Fairfax, VA.

Montaigne, M. "Of a monstrous child." Trans. Charles Cotton. 1580. *Quotidiana.* Ed. Patrick Madden, September 22, 2006, October 28, 2015. Retreived from http://essays.quotidiana.org/montaigne/monstrous_child/.

Morrison, T. (1987). *Beloved.* New York, NY: Alfred A. Knopf.

New Zealand Transport Agency (Producer). (2014). *Speed Ad – Mistakes* [Video file]. Retrieved from https://www.youtube.com/watch?v=bvLaTupw-hk.

Oliver, M. (1992). *Poetry 180: A Poem a Day for American High Schools.* Retrieved from http://www.loc.gov/poetry/180/124.html.

Orwell, G. (1950). *Shooting an Elephant and Other Essays.* New York: Harcout, Brace.

Ozar, K. [kevinozar]. (July 11, 2015). School is the real world for ss. Saying after grad = real world devalues what kids are feeling and doing in their lives and in class. [Tweet]. Retrieved from https://twitter.com/kevinozar/status/619921136311 214080?refsrc=email&s=11.

Reed, D. and Hicks, T. (2015). *Research Writing Rewired: Lessons that Ground Students' Digital Learning.* Thousand Oaks, CA: Corwin Literacy.

Robinson, K. (2011). *Out of Our Minds: Learning to be Creative.* Hoboken, NJ: Wiley.

Romano, T. (1987). *Clearing the Way: Working with Teenage Writers.* Portsmouth, NY: Heinemann.

Ronson, J. (2015). *So You've Been Publicly Shamed.* New York, NY: Riverhead Books.

Rosenwasser, D. and Stephen, J. (1997). *Writing Analytically.* Fort Worth, TX: Harcourt Brace College Publishers.

Rouner, J. (July 23, 2015). "No, it's not your opinion. You're just wrong" [updated]. *HoustonPress.* Retrieved from www.houstonpress.com.

Salinger, J. D. (1951). *The Catcher in the Rye.* Boston, MA: Little, Brown.

Siegel, H. (October 20, 2007). "Rowling lets dumbledore out of the closet." *abc-NEWS.* Retrieved from http://abcnews.go.com/Entertainment/story?id=3755544.

Smagorinsky, P. (2007). *Teaching English by Design: How to Create and Carry Out Instructional Units.* Portsmouth, NH: Heinemann.

Smith, M., Wilhelm, J. D., and Fredricksen, J. E. (2012). *Oh, Yeah?! Putting Argument to Work Both in School and Out.* Portsmouth, NH: Heinemann.

Spielberg, S. and Kennedy, K. (Producers), and Spielberg, S. (Director). (2002). *E.T. the Extra-Terrestrial* [Motion Picture]. United States: Universal Pictures.

Stephenson, N. (1999). *In the Beginning . . . was the Command Line.* New York, NY: Avon Books.

Stock, P. L. (1995). *The Dialogic Curriculum: Teaching and Learning in a Multicultural Society.* Portsmouth, NH: Heinemann.

Sullivan, A. (1999). "What's so bad about hate?" *The New York Times Magazine*, September 26, 1999.

Teachers Teaching Teachers. (n.d.). Retrieved from http://edtechtalk.com/ttt.

TED-Ed: Lessons Worth Sharing. (n.d.). Retrieved from http://ed.ted.com/.

Tomasco, S. (May 18, 2010). *IBM 2010 global CEO study: Creativity selected as most crucial factor for future success.* Retrieved November 2, 2015, from https://www-03.ibm.com/press/us/en/pressrelease/31670.wss.

Toulmin, S. (1958). *The Uses of Argument.* New York, NY: Cambridge University Press.

Virginia Department of Education. (2011). *End-of-Course Writing: 2010 English Standards of Learning.* Retrieved from http://www.doe.virginia.gov/testing/sol/blueprints/english_blueprints/2010/2010_blueprint_eoc_writing.pdf.

Virginia Department of Education. (2014). *End-of-Course Writing Prompts.* Retrieved from http://www.doe.virginia.gov/testing/sol/standards_docs/english/2010/online_writing/writing_prompts/eoc_writing_prompts.pdf.

Voluntaryist, C. (Publisher). (July 4, 2013). *4th of July DUI Checkpoint—Drug Dogs, Searched without Consent, While Innocent* [Video file]. Retrieved from https://www.youtube.com/watch?v=w-WMn_zHCVo&feature=youtu.be.

Wallace, D. F. (1996). "A supposedly fun thing I'll never do again." *Harper's Magazine.* Retrieved from http://harpers.org/wp-content/uploads/2008/09/HarpersMagazine-1996-01-0007859.pdf.

Wallace-Wells, B. (July 12, 2015). "The hard truths of Ta-Nehisi Coates." *New York Magazine.* Retrieved from http://nymag.com/daily/intelligencer/2015/07/ta-nehisi-coates-between-the-world-and-me.html?mid=twitter-share-di.

White, E. B. (1941). *Essays of E.B. White.* New York: Harper and Row, Publishers, Inc.

Whitney, A. E. (2011). "In search of the authentic English classroom: Facing the schoolishness of school." *English Education*, 44(1), 51–62.

Wiggins, G. P. and McTighe, J. (2005). *Understanding by Design* (Expanded 2nd ed.) Alexandria, VA: Association for Supervision and Curriculum Development, 2005. Print.

Wilhelm, J., Douglas, W., and Fry, S. (2014). *The Activist Learner: Inquiry, Literacy, and Service to Make Learning Matter.* New York: Teachers College, Columbia University.

Wilson, M. (2006). *Rethinking Rubrics in Writing Assessment.* Portsmouth, NH: Heinemann.

Winter, D. and Robbins, S. (Eds.). *Writing Our Communities: Local Learning and Public Culture.* Urbana, IL: National Council of Teachers of English and National Writing Project.

WOWK 13 News. (July 8, 2013). Retrieved from https://www.facebook.com/13news/?fref=ts.

Youth Voices. (n.d.). *What's Youth Voices all About?* Retrieved from http://youthvoices.net/about.

Index

About the Authors

Mitchell Nobis is an English teacher and department chair at Seaholm High School in Birmingham, Michigan. Mitchell is a co-director of the Red Cedar Writing Project at Michigan State University where his work revolves around the National Writing Project tenets that the best professional development is "teachers teaching teachers" and to best teach writing, teachers must be writers themselves. He is also the 2016 president of the Michigan Council of Teachers of English. In his spare time, he writes and plays basketball. He is in his twentieth year of teaching. Follow Mitch on Twitter at @MitchNobis.

Daniel Laird is in his sixteenth year as an English teacher at Leslie High School in Leslie, Michigan, and is also a teacher-consultant for the Red Cedar Writing Project, for which he is the co-director of the RCWP Greenrock Writers Retreat for writers in grades 8–12 as well as an instructor of various themed Spartan Writing Camps for writers in grades 6–8. He earned his master's degree in education with a focus on technology and learning from Michigan State University. Dan has conducted professional development for teachers in the area of argument writing and has been a resource provider for the National Writing Project's website *Digital Is*. Follow Dan on Twitter at @dandanlaird.

Carrie Nobis is an English, biology, and chemistry teacher at Groves High School in Beverly Hills, Michigan, and a teacher-consultant for the Red Cedar Writing Project at Michigan State University, where she is the co-director of the RCWP Greenrock Writers Retreat for writers in grades 8–12. She earned her master's degree in curriculum and teaching from Michigan State University. Carrie regularly invites her science students to use disciplinary literacy skills to deepen their understanding. She is in her fourteenth year of teaching, and earlier in her career, she taught in Detroit Public Schools and in an alternative high school in West Bloomfield, Michigan.

Dawn Reed is an English teacher at Okemos High School in Okemos, Michigan, and is currently in her eleventh year of teaching. She is a co-director of Red Cedar Writing Project at Michigan State University. Dawn earned her master's degree in writing and rhetoric with a specialization in critical studies in literacy and pedagogy from Michigan State University. She conducts professional development for teachers focused on technology integration and the teaching of writing. She is coauthor of *Research Writing Rewired: Lessons that Ground Students' Digital Learning* (Corwin Literacy 2015), and she has published in various journals, books, and websites. Follow Dawn on Twitter at @dawnreed.

Dirk Schulze is an English teacher at Lake Braddock Secondary School in Burke, Virginia, and a teacher-consultant with the Northern Virginia Writing Project. He earned his undergraduate degree from the University of Michigan, his master's degree in education from George Mason University, and was awarded National Board Certification in 2008. A former Outward Bound instructor, he is in his fifteenth year of high school teaching and strives to make his classroom a place where he and his students can take risks and learn from both their successes and their failures.